# guide to Andalucía

Text, photographs, design, lay-out and printing, entirely created by the technical department of EDITORIAL ESCUDO DE ORO, S.A.

Rights of total or partial reproduction and translation reserved.

Editorial Escudo de Oro, S.A.

## INTRODUCTION AND NOTES ON HOW TO USE THIS GUIDE

Andalusia, with an area of almost 90,000 km$^2$, is the largest Spanish region, as well as the most varied and unique due to its geographical diversity and its singular personality, the result of the passing through of many peoples. Bordered to the north by the Sierra Morena, Andalusia contains many different types of landscape, from almost desert areas to marshlands and rich farmlands, from beaches to the snows of the Sierra Nevada, from remote zones and isolated villages to the crowded Costa del Sol...

Throughout its history, Andalusia has been a cradle of civilisations and cultures. Settled since remote times, in around 700 BC, the mythical Tartessian people settled in the Guadalquivir Valley, succeeded by Phoenician and Greek colonies on the coast and Celts and Iberians inland. Later, the region was colonised by the Carthaginians, after which it was incorporated into the Roman Empire, when the regions of Hispania Ulterior and Bética Senatorial were established (2nd and 1st centuries BC).

A second era of splendour was ushered in by the Moorish invasion. Moorish domination spanned eight centuries (8th-15th) and gave a name to a new reality: Al-Andalus, the origins of the present-day name of Andalusia. This was the era of the Caliphate of Córdoba and, later, of the Kingdom of Granada. After the surrender of Granada, the last nucleus of Moorish resistance in Spain, in 1492, the Christian Reconquest was complete and Andalusia's fortunes came to depend on the Kingdom of Castile.

In 1492, Columbus inscribed another important historic event in the annals with the discovery of America. This caused the rapid development of Lower Andalusia, as in 1503 the *Casa de Contratación,* monopolising trade with the New World, was established in Seville. The cities of Seville and Cádiz became the busiest trading centres in Spain. Nevertheless, this did not lead to the complete dynamisation of the zone, and its standing in Spain actually declined.

The Andalusian community achieved great development, particularly in Seville and surrounding area, with the celebration in that city of the 1929 Ibero-American Exhibition and, above all, the 1992 Universal Exhibition, which entailed the construction of infrastructure such as the Technology Park and the High Speed Train (AVE) line.

Throughout history, then, different cultures have left their mark on the cities and villages, the gastronomy, the festivities and the personality of the people of Andalusia. It is said that it is made up of Castilian pride, Arabic pleasure in life, the peaceful wisdom of the Jews and the passion of the Gypsies.

In the pages of this guide, we shall try to show the reader some of the diversity of landscape and the magical attractions of Andalusia. The volume is divided into eight sections corresponding to each of the eight provinces forming the region. In each chapter, the first part is devoted to the capital of the province and the second to the environs or possible excursions from the capital. In both cases, a map is provided to help visitors find their way around. Routes and itineraries are also suggested in order to help tourists get the most out of their visit.

Due to their importance and enormous interest, the many and varied festivities of Andalusia are often dealt with in a special section. The Holy Week processions, particularly in Seville and Málaga, for instance, are famed all over the world. Another popular celebration is the *Fiesta de las Cruces* («Festival of the Crosses»), which achieves great splendour in Granada and Córdoba.

In spring and summer, many *romerías* (religious processions to sanctuaries) take place, outstanding among them being that of El Rocío (Our Lady of the Dew), which culminates in Almonte (Huelva), and that of Nuestra Señora de la Cabeza (Our Lady of the Head), near Andújar (Jaén). The exceptionally joyful and bustling April Fair in Seville will also captivate visitors.

Visitors to Andalusia should not miss the chance to try its rich gastronomy. Gazpacho, in its different presentations, is, without a doubt, the most universally known of Andalusian dishes, whilst seafood and fish dishes are hugely popular here. This is not to forget the excellent array of meat dishes: *estofado de rabo de toro* (bull tail stew), *riñones al jerez* (kidneys in sherry), game, etc. Also famed is the ham of Andalusia, as are the exquisite variety of cakes and desserts. As for the local wines and liqueurs, let us mention particularly those from Jerez, Huelva, Montilla and Moriles, and the sweet muscatels of Málaga, excellent as an aperitif or to accompany desserts.

*The cathedral and the Archivo de Indias building.*

## SEVILLE

More than one day is needed to get the most out of a visit to Seville, and the best thing is to take plenty of time and go about things calmly as we discover the rich heritage bequeathed by the long, eventful history of the city, enjoying its everyday enchantments and the character of its people. Below is a proposed itinerary around essential Seville, comprising, basically, of a tour of the historic city centre.

We begin at **La Giralda,** symbol of the city and one of the best-loved towers in the world. It was built in the 12th century and was the minaret of the Great Mosque, located on the site where the cathedral the now stands. The tower was then crowned by four great golden globes, which fell off during the 1356 earthquake. The Giralda is now completed by a bellchamber arranged in diminishing sections or kiosks, the work of Hernán Ruiz and which started to be built in 1558. At

*Cathedral: sacristia mayor.*

the very top is an enormous statute representing the Triumph of Faith, a weathercock which soon became known as El Giraldillo, the name from which that of the tower is derived. Inside, 35 gentle ramps lead up to a splendid viewpoint over the city, at a height of 70 metres.

**Seville Cathedral** is the largest in Spain and one of the biggest in the world: 130 metres in length and 76 in width with the highest point of the crossing reaching 56 metres. The basic body of the cathedral was constructed between 1420 and 1506, and it features Gothic, neo-Gothic and Renaissance elements. The dome which collapsed in 1511, was rebuilt in 1519 and renovated once more after the earthquake of 1888. The interior of the cathedral is impressive in its grandeur and solidity, as well as for the wealth of artistic works it contains, produced by some of the most outstanding artists. The cathedral has a nave and four aisles accommodating some 30 chapels. Of these, outstanding is the *Capilla Mayor,* presided

# CENTRE OF SEVILLE

1. The cathedral, the Giralda and the Patio de los Naranjos
2. Archbishop's palace
3. Plaza de Santa Marta
4. Casa Lonja - Archivo de Indias
5. Reales Alcázares
6. Santa Cruz district and square
7. Casa de Pilatos
8. City Hall
9. Church of El Salvador
10. Church of La Magdalena
11. Fine Art Museum
12. Real Maestranza bullring
13. Torre del Oro
14. Hospital de la Caridad
15. Palacio de San Telmo
16. University (formerly tobacco factory)
17. María Luisa Park
18. Prado de San Sebastián

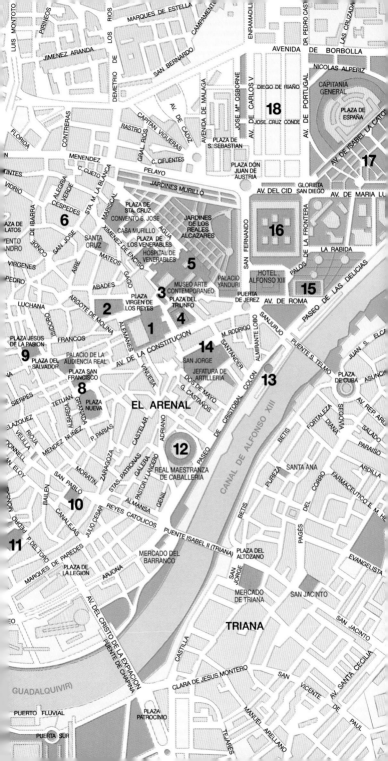

over by an immense altarpiece, a masterpiece of Flamboyant Gothic and closed by a fine 16th-century Plateresque grille. The Capilla Real contains the tombs of various monarchs and, in a magnificent silver urn, the mortal remains of King Ferdinand the Holy. Over the altar is the statue of the Virgen de los Reyes, patron saint of the city. The *Sacristia Mayor* contains the cathedral treasure, including the huge processional monstrance by Juan de Arfe, a unique example of Renaissance silverwork. The **Patio de los Naranjos,** formerly the *sahn* of the mosque, is surprising in its simple beauty. To the north is the Puerta del Perdón, one of the most interesting cathedral doors, dating back to the Almohade period. To the east, in the Aisle of El Lagarto, is the Columbine Library, founded in 1551, contain-

*Calle de la Judería in the Santa Cruz district.*

*Alcázar: Patio de la Montería.*

ing a priceless collection of manuscripts donated by the son of Christopher Columbus.

**Plaza Virgen de los Reyes** is the heart of monumental Seville. On one side is the cathedral and on the other the Archbishop's Palace with its lovely baroque front, whilst at a third corner a side-street leads to the recondite **Plaza de Santa Marta,** a particularly charming square. In nearby Plaza del Triunfo is the former **Casa Lonja** or **Archivo General de Indias,** a building constructed by Juan de Herrera in the 16th century. The «Archive of the Indias» was founded in 1785 by King Charles III to centralise the extensive documentation relating to the New World.

Of the original 12th-century Almohade **Alcázar,** all that remains is the Patio del Yeso and the Patio del Crucero. Its actual structure dates to the reign of Peter I, who used some of the elements of the original buildings. The Palace of King

*Plaza de Santa Cruz: the Cruz de Cerrajería.*

Don Pedro, a masterpiece of Mudéjar art, was built in the 14th century, though it was modified in subsequent periods. The most beautiful elements in the palace are the Patio de las Doncellas and that of Las Muñecas, the sumptuous Salón de Embajadores, the Oratorium of the Catholic Monarchs, and the gardens and environs, in Moorish, Mudéjar and Renaissance styles and featuring a maze.

The **Santa Cruz district** is reached from the Patio de Banderas, a vast space forming the Alcázar's parade ground. Santa Cruz still conserves the basic layout of what was formerly the Aljama, where the Jewish community later settled. It began to acquire part of its present physiognomy in the 16th century, when squares were built and streets widened. The style of this *barrio* was consolidated in the 19th century with the installation of gates allowing the inner courtyards to be admired from the street. The best way of getting to know this charming district is to lose oneself in its evocatively-named streets and squares: Callejón del Agua, Calle de Susona, Plaza de Doña Elvira, Plaza de los Venerables, Calle de Santa Teresa (with the Murillo house-museum) or Plaza de Santa Cruz, presided over by the Cruz de Cerrajería, an original wrought-iron cross dating to the year 1692.

Further on, starting at Calle Santa María la Blanca, extends the former San Bartolomé Jewish quarter, leading us into Plaza de Pilatos, occupied by the famous House of Pilate, built in the 15th and 16th centuries and of extraordinary interest due to its exquisite mixture of styles as varied as Renaissance, Mudéjar and Flamboyant Gothic.

We take up our route once more to visit Plaza de San Francisco and Plaza Nueva, nerve centre of the daily life of Seville. The latter contains the **City Hall,** a splendid example of Plateresque art, and forms the starting-point of the famous **Calle de las Sierpes,** the city's main artery. Nearby is the **Church of El Salvador,** a fine exponent of baroque art.

Heading now towards the river, we come to Plaza del Museo, containing the **Fine Art Museum** (Museo de Bellas Artes). The

*Fine Art Museum.*

*Overall view: Torre del Oro, San Telmo bridge and the Giralda.*

building it occupies was formerly a convent and was rebuilt in the 17th century. The quality and quantity of the treasures it houses makes it considered the second most important art museum in Spain, after the Prado. Its most outstanding collection is that devoted to the Seville School, featuring works by Pacheco, Zurbarán, Murillo, Roelas and Valdés Leal, amongst many more.

A winding route through different streets now brings us to Paseo de Cristóbal Colón, on the banks of the **Guadalquivir.** Due to constant flooding, the course of the river, which used to flow through the city, was altered in the middle of the present century, and what we now contemplate is the barest reminder of what this river once was, the arrival-point of the Conquistadores and symbol of the age of the discovery of America. Here, what used to be known as El Arenal, a zone surrounding what is now the Real Maestranza bullring and formerly a maritime

*Torre del Oro and Paseo de Cristóbal Colón.*

quarter, contained the shipyards where the vessels which plied the route to and from the New World were built.

The main entrance to the Real Maestranza bullring is in Paseo de Cristóbal Colón. This is, without a doubt, one of the most prestigious bullfighting venues in the world. Designed by Vicente San Martín, it was built in the 18th century. Seating 14,000 spectators, it is decorated in bright, cheerful colours. There is also a bullfighting museum and library.

The **Torre del Oro** is another of the most emblematic symbols of Seville. This is a twelve-sided Almohade tower dating back to the 13th century, though the turret which crowns it was added in 1760. Its name («Tower of Gold») is due to the fact that it was formerly covered in gilt tiles. The tower was connected by a thick chain to another tower, now lost, on the other side of the river, controlling traffic along the Guadalquivir. It also formed part of the old Moorish city walls, which stretched out as far as the

*Palacio de San Telmo: main front.*

Alcázar (the Torre de la Plata in Calle Santander and the Torre Abdelaziz at the end of this street, allow us to guess the full extension of this stretch of the walls). The Torre del Oro now houses a naval museum.

Behind the tower in Calle Temprado is the **Hospital de la Caridad.** This institution still functions as a nursing home for the elderly, and is one of the most impressive centres of art in the city, housing an excellent collection of paintings on the theme of death and misericord, featuring masterpieces by Valdés Leal and Murillo. Don Miguel de Mañara (18th century), after leading a dissolute life, devoted himself to this institution, directing the works of the hospital and the church, as well as personally organising the art collection which has brought the place renown.

Returning to the river bank, in Avenida de Roma, is the **Palacio de San Telmo,** whose construction began in 1682. This

*The former tobacco factory, now part of the university.*

palace features a fine Churrigueresque portal which contrasts with the general solemnity of the main front. It was originally a naval college (the central figure of the portal represents Saint Telmo, patron saint of navigation, surrounded by allegorical sculptures relating to nautical themes), and in 1848 became the residence of the Duke of Montpensier, pretender to the throne, until in 1901 it was donated by Princess Luisa to the archbishop, who installed the diocesan seminary here. It was acquired in 1992 by the autonomous government of Andalusia for conversion into the offices of the presidency.

What is now the **University** building was constructed between 1728 and 1771 to replace the tobacco factory which stood in the city centre and which had become too small. As this was a public building, it was designed in the form of a citadel, explaining why it contains a prison, moat and drawbridge: the tobacco industry was then very powerful and the factory

*Plaza de España.*

therefore had a permanent guard over it to prevent smuggling and black marketeering. The «Fábrica de Tabacos» enjoyed a monopoly in the production of tobacco and was for many years the most prosperous industry in Seville, employing the biggest workforce, amongst its workers being Carmen, the popular cigar-maker who inspired Merimée's novel of the same name. The building take the shape of a rectangle measuring 250 by 180 metres and was divided into two areas; the residential section and the factory itself.

We now enter the **Parque de María Luisa** through Glorieta de San Diego, the main entrance for the Ibero-American Exhibition in 1929. This magnificent, leafy park, especially pleasant during the hot summer months, was donated to the city by Princess Doña Luisa in 1893 and was later transformed into a trade fair venue for the Exhibition, a restructuring involving the construction of pavilions and squares. Among these, particu-

*Mudéjar pavilion in Plaza de América.*

larly interesting are the **Plaza de España,** a 200-meter diameter semicircle in which all the Spanish provinces are represented in the benches lining it; Plaza de América, containing
the **Pabellón Real** (Royal Pavilion), a construction in
Flamboyant Gothic style; the **Pabellón Plateresco,** or
**Renacentista** (Plateresque or Renaissance Pavilion), which
now houses the Archaeological Museum, one of the foremost
museums of its kind in Spain, its collections including the
extraordinary Carambolo Treasure, a jewel going back to the
times of the Tartessian culture; and the **Pabellón Mudéjar,**
since 1972 the seat of the Popular Arts and Customs Museum.
Plaza de América connects with Paseo de la Palmera, one of
the city's most beautiful promenades, lined with noble houses
and other former pavilions, among them the singularly interesting Mexican, Moroccan and Peruvian pavilions. The park
also contains a number of *glorietas* (summer houses), the

*Holy Week: the Cristo Nazareno.*

most popular being that dedicated to the Sevillian poet Gustavo Adolfo Bécquer, by Coullaut Varela (1912).

**Holy Week** in Seville is a unique spectacle, reaching heights of intensity and emotion that the visitor can only understand by sharing it with the people of the city. For the Sevillian, this is the great *fiesta,* the most popular, a passion. Its origins go back to the 16th century and there now exist around 50 *cofradías,* or brotherhoods, which parade some 100 pasos, floats, in the processions. These take place every day during Holy Week - seven or eight brotherhoods taking part each day - in the evening and at night, as they take around 12 hours to complete their route. Programmes are sold in the streets and local newspapers give timetables, itineraries and other information.

The processions begin at the churches where the brotherhoods have their seats. They go to the cathedral and back again by a different route. Each brotherhood, whose members wear a different costume, usually carries two *pasos,* sculptural groups, the first representing an image of the Passion and the second a Dolorosa, or statue of the Virgin affected by the pain of the death of Jesus. These floats are carried on the shoulders to a rhythm marked by the voice of a *capataz.* The heads of the penitents accompanying them are hooded and they carry a candle in their hands. The carvings are often veritable works of art, most dating to the 17th century, the figures richly dressed and adorned, particularly the Virgins. A spectacular atmosphere is created by all this, the crowds and the perfumed aroma of flowers, incense and candles.

During **Corpus Christi,** which takes place at the end of May or during the first fortnight of June, the procession starts out from the cathedral and goes around some of the streets of the centre, preceded by Juan de Arfe's great processional monstrance and followed by various pasos and representatives of Sevillian civil and religious society. The events also

*Virgen del Mayor Dolor and Traspaso.*

*Caseta at the April Fair.*

feature the dances of the «seises» («sixes») in front of the high altar in the cathedral. The dance resembles a slow minuet and is interpreted by young people dressed in the costume of the 17th century.

After the solemnity of Holy Week, the city explodes into joy during the April Fair. This takes place during the second half of April and lasts one week. This is a secular, country-style festivity which was first staged in 1848, though its origins are a cattle market which used to be held here. A great entrance archway lit up by hundreds of lightbulbs beckons us into an enclosure full of canvas stands put up by the different participation associations. Inside, the fun and dancing of Sevillanas goes on to the early hours, whilst outside horsemen parade their ornately-harnessed steeds, the women wearing their finest dresses.

The pilgrimage known as the **Romería del Rocío** takes place at Whitsun. The tradition began in the early-18th century and

*The religious procession, or* romería, *for the Virgen del Rocío.*

the pilgrimage is made by Sevillians and visitors alike, culmi-
nating at the Hermitage of El Rocío near Almonte (Huelva). The
route from Seville covers 95 kilometres and the journey is
made in carts pulled by oxen, on horseback or on foot. Well-
organised groups accompany and escort the Carro del
Sinpecado («cart of the Sinless One») which identifies each
brotherhood. The procession reaches the hermitage on Whit
Saturday and the offering is made to the Virgin, popularly
known as La Blanca Paloma («The White Dove»), faithfully
watched over by the Matriz de Almonte brotherhood. On the
Sunday, a solemn mass is held, and at night a public prayer
service is held. In the early hours of Monday, the people of
Almonte, the only ones with this privilege, jump over the grille
and carry the statue of the Virgin out in procession. As one, the
multitude acclaims the Virgin, crowding round to try to touch
the silver poles of the float.

*Map of Seville province.*

## ENVIRONS OF SEVILLE

Some ten kilometres from the capital is **Santiponce,** whose main attraction is the Monastery of San Isidoro del Campo, founded by Alonso Pérez de Guzmán in the early-14th century. The monastery features works by Martínez Montañés (17th century), including the altarpiece and the tombs of Guzmán the Good and his wife.

Near to Santiponce are the ruins of **Itálica,** a Roman city founded in 203 BC by Scipio Africanus. Originally a military encampment, it developed into a prosperous city, the birthplace of Trajan and Hadrian, this last responsible for the monumental wealth Itálica boasted. However, the city was first abandoned and then sacked in later periods, becoming a ghost city, its glorious past forgotten. The visitor can now admire the city's layout, completely regular and systematic, as well as the remains of mosaics and sculptures. A small museum exhibits a collection of findings, though many pieces are now in the Archaeological Museum in Seville. Nevertheless, the ruins of Itálica still conserve such impressive vestiges as the amphitheatre, elliptical in shape and holding 25,000 spectators, and the theatre.

Taking the Córdoba road, we now come to **Carmona,** some 35 kilometres from Seville. This is a town of great interest due to its wealth of monuments. Of its Roman past remain stretches of wall, the amphitheatre and the necropolis, but it was under the Moorish domination that Carmona achieved its greatest splendour. To this period belong the foundations of the Alcázar and the town centre which, though added to in later years, still maintains a strongly Oriental character.

During the 17th and 18th centuries, many convents and palaces were built in Carmona. The Palacio de los Aguilar and the Palacio de los Rueda are two fine exponents of baroque architecture, whilst the most impressive of the town's religious

*Ruins of Italica: amphitheatre.*

*Carmona: Calle Pedro I.*

buildings are the Church of Santa María, built in the 15th century over the site of the old mosque, of which are conserved the courtyard of ablutions; the Convent of Santa Clara and the Church of San Felipe, both Mudéjar in style; and the Church of San Pedro, whose tower is reminiscent of the Giralda in Seville.

Not far from Carmona is **Mairena de Alcor,** perched on a peak commanding fine views. Of remote origins, the town's present physiognomy is Moorish. The so-called Castillo de Luna («Moon Castle») also dates back to the period of Moorish splendour in Andalusia. It is now in a good state of repair and has an interesting Archaeological Museum. Other points of interest are the Mudéjar Church of La Asunción and the hermitages of El Cristo de la Cárcel and San Sebastián.

The charm of **Écija** lies in the overall appearance of the city itself, its white houses with grilled windows and ochre roofs

*Mairena de Alcor: Luna castle.*

and its many churches and palatial houses. Plaza de España, the nerve centre and main meeting-place, is known as «El Salón», and Écija is also known as «the city of the towers», possessing twelve, the finest that of the Church of San Juan, and as «the frying-pan of Andalusia» due to the high temperatures reached here in summer. Its chief monuments include the Palacio de Peñaflor, also known as «the house of the long balconies», the Convent of Las Teresas, formerly a palatial mansion, and the Palacio de Benajemí, whose stables have been converted into a carriage museum. All these buildings are catalogued as National Monuments.

In **Marchena** is conserved part of the old Almohade town, including the urban layout and the city walls, including the gate known as the Arch of the Rose. In Plaza Ducal stand the tower of the old Alcazaba, the Mudéjar courtyard and the Chapterhouses. Nevertheless, Marchena's principal feature

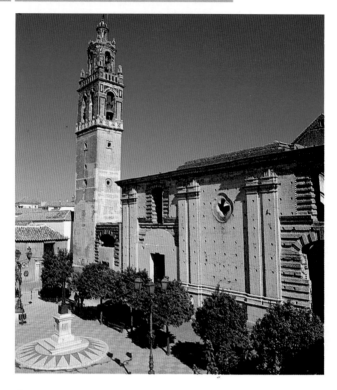

*Écija.*

are its churches, of which there are many, built between the 15th and 18th centuries. In the Gothic-Mudéjar Church of San Juan Bautista is a beautiful baroque altarpiece, the work of Alejo Fernández, and a museum containing paintings by Zurbarán.

The city of **Osuna,** with its noble past as the seat of a duchy, is a site of enormous historic and artistic interest. Founded by the Iberians, it reached its period of maximum splendour when Philip II gave the Count of Ureña the title of Duke of Osuna in the 16th century. To this century date the city's principal monuments, such as the splendid Collegiate Church of Santa María de la Asunción (containing an excellent collection of paintings), the University and the Pantheon of the Dukes of Osuna. The Torre del Agua, a 12th-century Almohade tower, houses an Archaeological Museum displaying Iberian, Roman and Visigoth items. In the outskirts of the city are the remains of a Roman circus and necropolis.

*Marchena.*

*Osuna.*

*Torre de la Calahorra.*

## CORDOBA

Córdoba is a city rich in art and history. Its period of greatest splendour occurred during the times of Moorish rule, when it became the capital of the Western world. A walk around the environs of the mosque and the narrow streets of the old Jewish quarter is enough to evoke this glorious past in the mind of the visitor, though Córdoba also offers many more attractions, and more than a day should be spent here in order to appreciate the city.

We begin our tour at the **Torre de la Calahorra.** Originally a Moorish tower, the construction we can now contemplate dates to the year 1369. It was declared a monument of historic and artistic interest in 1931 and since 1987 has housed a museum devoted to Córdoba during the Caliphate, sponsored by the Roger Garaudy Foundation and dedicated to the three cultures which lived together here: the Moorish, the Jewish and the Christian.

We reach the city by crossing the **Roman bridge,** built during the reign of Emperor Augustus and which formed part of the Via Augusta, though only the foundations remain of this original construction. The bridge features a statue of Saint Raphael, an image which appears again and again in the city, forming part of its physiognomy. Popular adoration of this archangel, patron saint of the city, dates back to the 16th century, though most of the monuments dedicated to the saint are 17th- and 18th-century and are known as *triunfos,* commemorating as they do Raphael's glory. The **Triunfo de San Rafael** adjoining the **Puerta del Puente** is by Michel de Verdiguier and is the most typical in the entire city. The triumphal arch known as the Puerta del Puente was designed by Juan Herrera in 1571, though the original was built the during times of the Roman empire.

Next, we walk around the mosque walls to the north side, where we find the Patio de los Naranjos entrance. The mosque of Córdoba, symbol of the city's period of maximum splendour, is also a demonstration of the superimposition of the civilisations which have predominated here, dating back to

*Mosque: east and south fronts.*

# CORDOBA

1. Torre de la Calahorra
2. Roman bridge
3. Puerta del Puente
4. Triunfo de San Rafael
5. Albolafia mill
6. Calleja de las Flores
7. Mosque and Cathedral
8. Episcopal Palace
9. Portada de San Jacinto
10. Alcázar de los Reyes Cristianos
11. Puerta de Sevilla
12. Puerta de Almodóvar
13. Synagogue
14. City Bullfighting Museum
15. Chapel of San Bartolomé
16. Casa del Indiano
17. Church of San Nicolás de la Vila
18. Church of San Miguel
19. Roman temple
20. Cristo de los Faroles
21. Palacio de la Diputación
22. Torre de la Malmuerta
23. Plaza de la Corredera
24. Church of San Pedro
25. Julio Romero de Torres Museum and
   Fine Art Museum
26. Posada del Potro
27. Church of San Francisco
28. Arco del Portillo
29. Archaeological Museum
30. Church of Santa Marina de las Aguas
31. Palacio de Viana
32. Church of San Agustín
33. Church of San Lorenzo
34. Church of La Magdalena
35. Church of San Andrés
36. Church of San Pablo

*Mosque: aisles of Abderramán II.*

Roman times. This is now a heterogeneous building made up of two magnificent oratories which are very different one from another. As a mosque, it is the largest in the Western world, with a total area of almost 24,000 m². It is also, along with the Medina Azahara city-palace on the outskirts of the city, the most important work of what is known as Caliphal art.

From outside, the most imposing feature of the mosque is its towered walls, fortified by square turrets and in which are the openings of many gates. On the north side we also find a tiny altar devoted to the «Virgen de los Faroles», particularly charming at night, when it is lit up. The visit to the aljama mosque begins at the Puerta del Perdón, a Mudéjar gate dating back to the 15th century. The Patio de los Naranjos is particularly attractive in spring, when it is filled by the perfume of the flowers which give it its name («Courtyard of the Orange Trees»). The minaret, now belltower, was built during the reign of Abderramán III, though later restoration has concealed its original structure.

The mosque was extended three times to keep up with the growing population of the city. It was originally constructed under Abderramán I and had eleven aisles. Abderramán II carried out the first extension (833-852), the part most affected by the later construction of the cathedral, whilst the second and most interesting was carried out during the reign of Alhakem II (961-966). The minister Almanzor ordered the final, most austere of these extensions, which almost doubled the mosque in size, in the year 987. In all, the prayer hall featured over one thousand pillars, of which 850 remained after the reforms to incorporate the various Christian churches were complete.

For the original construction, columns, capitals and stones were brought from different and remote places. The arches, Moorish on the lower level and semicircular above, are Visigoth in origin and are made up of red brick and white stone voussoirs, which give the building its peculiar two-tone effect.

*Mosque: aisles of Alhakem II and the mihrab.*

*Cathedral: crossing and high altar.*

Arches were superimposed one on another in order to raise and lighten the building, as well as to let in light from the exterior. The Alhakem II extension is considered the finest exponent of Caliphal art. The most spectacular elements are the trifoiled arches and, especially, the *mihrab,* an exquisitely beautiful element, a decorative and architectural marvel.

After the Christian Reconquest, the mosque was consecrated as the Cathedral of Santa María Mayor, and a series of reforms were carried out right up to the 16th century to adapt the building to Christian worship, though the new decoration harmonised with the Moorish elements and conserved the perspective of the original mosque, as in the case of the **Chapel of Villaviciosa** (15th century), featuring a splendid dome, or the **Capilla Real** (13th century), built in Mudéjar style. The **cathedral** began to built in 1523, though not without controversy due to the strong opposition brought to bear by various important personages. The Christian monument is in itself an admirable architectural and decorative achievement, though its peculiar situation takes away much of its interest. Originally designed in Gothic style, Mudéjar, Plateresque and Isabelline influences can also be seen in it. The 18th-century choirstalls are carved in mahogany from the Indies. Also baroque in style are the pulpits, carved by Michel de Verdiguier. The altarpiece, built using Carcabuey marble, features paintings by Antonio de Palomino and gilt wooden carvings by Pedro de Paz.

Opposite the mosque in Calle Torrijos is the **Episcopal Palace** (Palacio Episcopal), formerly residence of the Omeya caliphs but completely reformed in the 16th century. It now houses the Diocesan Art Museum and contains an interesting collection from the heritage of the Catholic Church of Córdoba from

*The gardens of the Alcázar de los Reyes Cristianos.*

*Puerta de Almodóvar and monument to Seneca.*

medieval times to the present day. Adjoining it is the **Palace of Congresses and Exhibitions** (Palacio de Congresos y Exposiciones) occupying various historic buildings, and the **Chapel of San Jacinto,** featuring a fine Gothic-Plateresque portal.

The **Alcázar de los Reyes Cristianos** was the royal residence from the late-13th century. After the surrender of Granada in 1492, the Catholic Monarchs gave it to the Courts of the Holy Office, which occupied it until the abolition of the Inquisition in 1821. In 1951 it passed into the possession of the city council, which restored it to its original character as a medieval palace. The building contains Roman works such as sarcophagi and mosaics, all magnificent pieces. Nevertheless, the main attraction of the Alcázar resides in its splendid gardens in which, as is traditional in Moorish gardens, water is a key protagonist. Nearby are the remains of the old city **walls.** Some of the city gates also survive: the 10th-century **Puerta de Sevilla** with its identical arches, and the **Puerta de Almodóvar,** possibly built in the 14th century though restored in the 19th. This route leads us past various monuments to illustrious Cordobans: the poet Aben Hazam (994-1064), Averröes (1126-1198), the Moorish philosopher who introduced Aristotelian thought to the Western world; and Seneca (4 BC to 65 AD).

The **Puerta de Almodóvar** provides entry to the old **Jewish quarter,** extending east of the mosque. In order to get to know historic Córdoba, it is essential to wander through this veritable labyrinth of narrow, winding streets. The best way is to lose oneself, discovering at each step picturesque corners and fine buildings and monuments. In Calle Judíos we come to the **synagogue,** dating back to the early-15th century, the only one from these times to have survived in Andalusia. Small, and with a square groundplan, the building is decorated with fine plasterwork and inscriptions from the Hebrew Psalms. The **Zoco,** installed in a Mudéjar building, offers a wide variety of samples of Cordoban craftwork. In Plazuela de Tiberiades is a monument to Maimonides (1135-1205), the famous Jewish

*The synagogue.*

*Cordoban patio.*

philosopher and doctor. The adjoining Plaza de las Bulas contains the entrance to the **Municipal Taurine Museum,** dedicated to the great Cordoban bullfighters. In Calle de Cardenal Salazar, adjoining the former Hospital de Agudos, is the **Chapel of San Bartolomé,** a lovely exponent of the Gothic-Mudéjar style, and in Plaza Angel Torres we find the house known as the **Casa del Indiano,** the ground floor built in Mudéjar style and the first floor in Isabelline. Other sights of great charm include the famous **Calleja de las Flores,** offering lovely views of the cathedral tower, and Calle Encarnación or the narrow Calleja del Pañuelo.

Though most of the houses in the old Jewish quarter are modest and relatively small, all of them give onto beautiful patios. The origins of the **Cordoban patio** go back to Roman times, when houses were arranged around an open space used as an agora, and to the Moorish period when, although the palaces and cities had their own patios, the model of the Roman house continued to be followed, with the addition of flowerbeds and water in the shape of a well or fountain. Nevertheless, we can distinguish two types of patio, the aristocratic and the popular. These courtyards achieve their maximum splendour during the Cordoban patio competition, which takes place during the May Festivals.

In Plaza Jerónimo Páez, on the site of the former palace of the Páez de Castillejo family, is the Archaeological Museum. Sumptuous staircases, rich coffering and lovely aristocratic patios make a visit to this museum - one of the most important of its kind in Spain - a pure delight. The items displayed in the museum include pieces from the Neolithic and Iberian periods, a fine collection of mosaics and many pieces from the Visigoth period. There is a splendid collection of pieces dating back to Moorish times, including an inlaid bronze stag from the Medina Azahara.

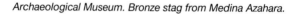

*Archaeological Museum. Bronze stag from Medina Azahara.*

*Plaza del Potro.*

Heading towards Plaza del Potro, we now come to the **Arco del Portillo,** an entrance opened in the inner walls of the city in the 14th century to communicate the «Almedina» with the «Axerquía», that is, the high and low districts of the city. Almost opposite this archway is the **Church of San Francisco,** with an entry archway and small garden. This was formerly a convent founded by Ferdinand III, the Holy, and of which the medieval cloisters are conserved.

The **Plaza del Potro** is one of the most seductive corners of Córdoba. During the 15th and 16th centuries it was the meeting-point for merchants and travellers from all over the Peninsula, the refuge of rogues and a labour exchange. Its present name was given to it in 1577, when the famous fountain was installed here, crowned by a rearing *potro* (colt) bearing the coat of arms of the city. At one end of the square is yet another *triunfo de San Rafael,* whilst on one side is the historic inn known as the **Posada del Potro,** conserved almost intact since the time when it was immortalised by Cervantes in his *Don Quijote and Rinconete and Cortadillo*. On the opposite side is the old building of the **Hospital de la Caridad,** now seat of the Julio Romero de Torres and Fine Art museums. ...

A small gardened patio containing various sculptures forms the antechamber to the two museums. The **Fine Art Museum** section is housed principally in the former church of the hospital. It has an excellent collection of paintings by various artists, as well as an important series of works by the Cordoban sculptor Mateo Inurria and collections of engravings and drawings.

The **Julio Romero de Torres Museum** is the most popular in the city in terms of numbers of visitors, drawn here by the personality and artistry of this well-known painter. This museum and house has over 50 of Romero's works, as well as many of his personal belongings. The work of Julio Romero de

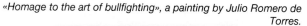

*«Homage to the art of bullfighting», a painting by Julio Romero de Torres.*

*Plaza de la Corredera.*

Torres is inspired in the artist's native Córdoba and takes as its main theme the female figure, with portraits full of sensuality. Romero was a very successful and popular painter in his time, often causing controversy due to the theme of many of his works. «La Chiquita Piconera», «Oranges and Lemons», «Poem to Córdoba» and «Offering to the Art of Bullfighting» are just a few of the interesting works by this «painter of dark women», as the popular song calls him.

Calle Armas and Calle Sánchez Peña lead us now to **Plaza de la Corredera.** This square is what is known as «Castilian» in style, and is the only one of its kind in Andalusia. Its present structure dates back to the late-17th century, when it was transformed in order to provide the city with a suitable arena for the staging of events of various types (masquerades, autos-da-fé, executions and bullfights, etc). It currently accommodates the stalls of a small market. Under the arcades and in the surrounding streets are traditional old inns and taverns which have retained their typical structure. Not far from the square are the columns of a small 1st-century **Roman temple.**

We now take Calle Capitulares and Calle Alfaros to La Cuesta del Bailío, entering Plaza de los Dolores, also known as Plaza de Capuchinos, by a narrow street. This is a simple square, impressive in its silence. In the centre, like an abandoned *paso,* or processional float, is **El Cristo de los Faroles,** whose name («the Christ of the Lamps») alludes to the eight lamps which, in the form of iron flowers, illuminate this statue of the Crucifixion. The statue was placed here in 1794, since when it has been the subject of pious popular devotion. The buildings surrounding the square are the 17th-century Capuchins' Convent, the Hospital of San Jacinto, founded in 1596, and the Church of Los Dolores, built in the 18th century. This peaceful church contains one of the statutes most revered by the faithful of Córdoba, that of the Virgin of Los Dolores, carved by the Granada-born sculptor Juan Prieto in 1719.

*Cristo de los Faroles.*

*Palace of the Provincial Government.*

In contrast to tiny Plaza de los Dolores, the nearby Plaza de Colón is one of the broadest squares in Córdoba. It is also known by the name of Campo de la Merced in allusion to the former Convent of the Mercedarians, now **Palace of the Provincial Government** (Palacio de la Diputación Provincial). The convent, founded by King Ferdinand, was completely rebuilt in the 18th century and represents the finest baroque work in the city. It features a broad front of bright colours and, inside, a lovely main staircase, as well as various patios, especially the central courtyard, in Renaissance style. The church has a majestic portal and contains a magnificent altarpiece with sculptures by Gómez Sandoval, considered the finest altarpiece in Córdoba, though presently being restored after being damaged by fire.

At one end of Plaza de Colón stands the **Torre de la Malmuerta,** now restored to good condition. According to the inscriptions under the arch of this tower, it was built between 1406 and

1408 by order of Henry III of Castile, and formed, without doubt, part of the old city walls. This thick-walled octagonal tower has such Mudéjar elements as the finely-worked band supporting the battlements. Its name («Tower of the Wrongly Killed») refers to a popular legend of a nobleman who killed his wife, accusing her of adultery. Apprised of her innocence, he begged pardon of the king and was condemned to built the tower in memory of «La Malmuerta».

In Plaza de Don Gome stands the **Palacio de Viana.** This was a lordly mansion which belonged to various families over time, being extended by the construction of adjoining houses. The site now covers a total area of 6,500 m² with 14 patios, all of exquisite beauty and one of the main attractions of this palace. Now converted into a museum, conserving the atmosphere of the period, its various rooms contain collections of tapestries, paintings, jewellery, porcelain services, furniture, etc. There is also a complete collection of embossed and Cordoban leather goods, as well as an extensive library, rich, particularly, in books on hunting.

*Torre de la Malmuerta.*

*Church of Santa Marina de Aguas Santas and monument to the bullfighter Manolete.*

This area of the city also contains various religious buildings, many of them dating back to the time of the Reconquest. Once the city had fallen into the hands of Ferdinand the Holy and the mosque had been consecrated as a cathedral, it was established that fourteen parish churches should be built in the city, as well as various convents, and this work was carried out between the late-13th and early-14th centuries. Sometimes known as *Fernandinas,* these churches feature Romanesque and Gothic elements along with Mudéjar touches, though many were later restored in baroque style. One of the most interesting of these religious buildings is the **Church of Santa Marina de Aguas Santas,** which has the aspect of a fortress. Opposite this building is a **monument to Manolete.** Manuel Rodríguez, «Manolete», (1917-1947) grew up in the Santa Marina district of the city. The son and grandson of bullfighters, he first entered the ring in Córdoba in 1939, immediately establishing himself as a leading figure. Due to his courage and professional honour, Manolete became a legendary figure, reinforced by his death in the bullring in Linares, gored by the bull «Islero».

Other Fernandine churches include those of **San Agustín,** all that remains of a Dominican convent; **San Lorenzo,** characterised by the porch at the main entrance, an infrequent element in Andalusian religious architecture; **La Magdalena,** a Gothic edifice; **San Pablo,** containing a masterpiece of Spanish statue-making, «Nuestra Señora de las Angustias» by Juan de Mesa; **San Miguel,** a Gothic-Romanesque work conserving a fine portal bearing influences of the Caliphal style; and **San Nicolás de la Villa,** outstanding particularly due to its elegant tower.

One of the liveliest areas of the city is **Plaza de las Tendillas,** the pulsating heart of Córdoba and meeting-point for locals and visitors alike. In Roman times, this was the focal point of the city, though its present structure corresponds to the

*Church of San Lorenzo.*

*High-Speed Train (AVE) station.*

beginnings of this century. In the centre is a monument to «El Gran Capitán», an outstanding military leader during the Christian Reconquest.

Though, once it had lost its Caliphal splendour, Córdoba began to be considered a mere place of transit the 20th century has represented a period of modernisation and the development of a complete and varied offer of services, as well as the establishment of the city as an important centre of communications between the south of Spain and the rest of Europe, a role further heightened recently with the construction of motorways and the High-Speed Train (AVE) station. All this has seen the city continue to grow, embellished by wide avenues and numerous parks and gardens.

Regarding local festivities, **Holy Week** has a long tradition in Córdoba and is celebrated with great splendour. There are some 28 *cofradías* (brotherhoods) in the city, possessing a total of around 50 *pasos,* or processional floats. The processions start out in the respective district and the official route includes Calle Claudio Marcelo and Plaza de las Tendillas, continuing along Calle Gondomar and Calle del Gran Capitán. Various festivities take place in May: the **Fiesta de la Cruz,** during which magnificent floral crosses compete for beauty, the **Cordoban Patio Competition,** a unique opportunity for visitors, as the locals open the doors of their houses to allow access to their patios, and the **Feria de la Salud,** a fair which takes place in the Arenal district and which is complemented, amongst other events, by bullfights in the Plaza de los Califas.

*Fiesta de la Cruz.*

*Map of Córdoba province.*

## ENVIRONS OF CORDOBA

The environs of Cordoba, the countryside to the south and the mountains to the north, give the visitor the chance to make enjoyable excursions to enjoy different types of scenery. The Sierra also contains a number of sites of outstanding interest, the most important of them without doubt the palace city of **Medina Azahara,** just ten kilometres from the city centre.

Considered the «Versailles of Caliphal Art» due to its rich, sumptuous features the life of this magnificent architectural site was as splendid as it was brief. Construction began in 936 under Abderramán III, first Caliph of Al-Andalus, in honour of his favourite, Al Zahra, and was finally completed 25 years later by the Caliph's son, Alhakem II. The walled site occupied over one thousand hectares and was built by the finest artists of the day, using the richest materials. However, in 1010, the city was sacked and destroyed in the course of the Fitna, the civil war which caused the break-up of the Caliphate into smaller *taifas,* kingdoms. Later, materials from it were even used in the construction of local buildings. The arduous work of reconstruction presently being undertaken means that visitors can now form an idea of the original splendour of this magnificent site.

Near to Medina Azahara is the **Monastery of San Jerónimo de Valparaíso,** founded in the early 15th-century. Conserved of the original building are the chapterhouse, the prior's cell and the Gothic cloister, a two-storey construction of austere beauty. The church was completely reformed during the baroque period.

In the Sierra are the **hermitages of Córdoba.** The present hermitages were built between 1703 and 1709, though their origins go back to the 4th century. A visit to these peaks is made worthwhile just by the magnificent views they command.

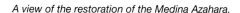

*A view of the restoration of the Medina Azahara.*

*The Albaicín and the Alhambra.*

## GRANADA

Known as one of the world's most beautiful cities, thanks to the splendour of its monuments and its magnificent situation between the plains and the Alhambra and Albaicín hills at the foot of the snowy peaks of the Sierra Nevada and close to the sea, the atmosphere of Granada seduces the visitor, with its evocation of its Moorish past when it was capital of the Nasrite kingdom. This, we should recall, is the only city of the Iberian Peninsula which was wholly Moslem during the Middle Ages, and was the last centre of resistance in Spain until it finally surrendered in 1492.

Seen from the outside, the **Alhambra** appears surprisingly austere, giving no hint of the treasures that await the visitor once inside its walls. This architectural marvel, formerly the residence of the Nasrite dynasty, is made up of a series of palaces, gardens, turrets and walls built in different epochs: in the 9th century there stood here a simple fortress to which Mohammed Ibn Al-Ahmar (1232-1272), founder of the dynasty, transferred his residence from the nearby Albaicín hill. The principal works, however, were carried out during the reigns of Yusuf I (1333-1354) and his son, Mohammed V (1354-1391). The Catholic Monarchs carried out a number of modifications, and Charles V later built the Renaissance palace which bears his name.

Artistically speaking, the Alhambra is a work of Nasrite or Granada art, characterised above all by an extraordinary aesthetic refinement. The site dates back to the 14th and 15th centuries, a period during which the Moorish empire on the Peninsula was in decline politically and, more than building for posterity, the Nasrites sought to give expression to the greatest possible luxury and sumptuousness, the decorative element forming the base of the magnificent beauty of the Alhambra.

The visit to the Alhambra begins at the **Puerta de las Granadas,** reached from Plaza Nueva at the end of Cuesta de Gomérez.

*Alhambra: Patio of the Lions.*

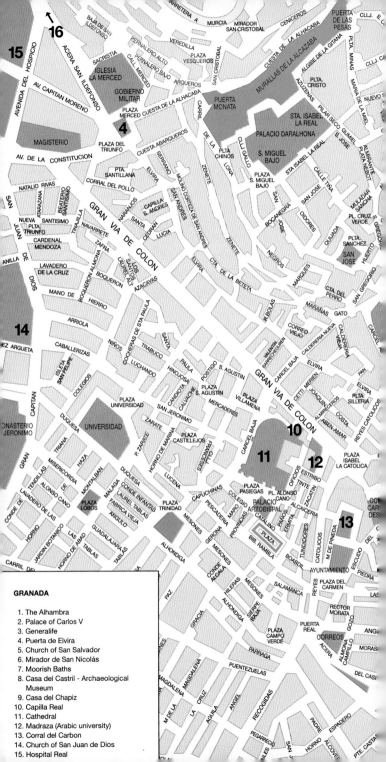

**GRANADA**

1. The Alhambra
2. Palace of Carlos V
3. Generalife
4. Puerta de Elvira
5. Church of San Salvador
6. Mirador de San Nicolás
7. Moorish Baths
8. Casa del Castril - Archaeological Museum
9. Casa del Chapiz
10. Capilla Real
11. Cathedral
12. Madraza (Arabic university)
13. Corral del Carbon
14. Church of San Juan de Dios
15. Hospital Real

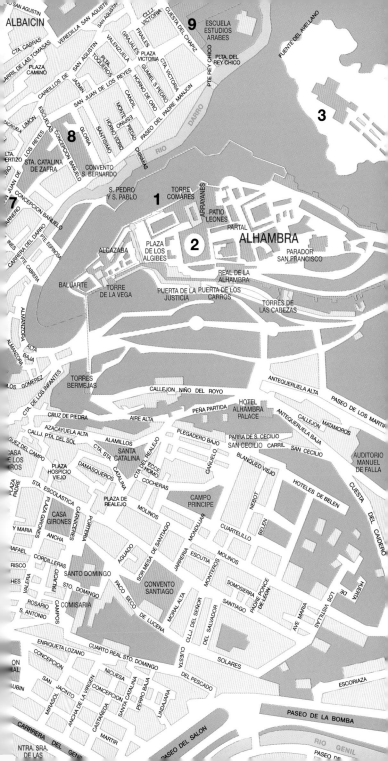

*Entrance to the Torre de Comares in the Patio of the Myrtles.*

This gate, by Pedro Maxuca, dates to the 16th century. To the right are the **Torres Bermeja,** built in the 11th century. Once we have passed through the gate we are confronted by the **Alamedas de la Alhambra,** tree-lined gardens installed here in the 16th century on the site of what were formerly defensive areas. A path leads to the main entrance, the **Puerta de la Justicia,** with a great Moorish arch built in the time of Yusuf I and, next to it, the **Pilar de Carlos V,** a lovely Renaissance fountain whose spouts represent the three rivers of Granada: the Beyro, the Darro and the Genil. A zig-zagging tunnel now leads us to the **Plaza de los Aljibes,** from where we can enter the Alcazaba, the original nucleus of the Alhambra, created by Mohammed Ibn Al-Ahmar, first Nasrite king. Here stands the famous **Torre de la Vela,** a tower built by the Catholic Monarchs offering magnificent views over the city.

Whilst the Alcazaba, as a former military zone, is practically bare of all decoration, the **Nasrite palaces** are characterised by an rich and exquisite ornamental quality. The palace complex can be divided into three main areas: the **Mexuar,** which held the dependencies of the legal administration, the Palacio de Comares (built by Yusuf I) and the Palacio de los Leones (by Mohammed V), containing the official residence of the king and the private apartments.

The Mexuar consists of the former Council Chamber («Sala de Consejos»), converted into a **chapel** in 1629 and whose original decorative elements are mixed with later additions such as coats of arms and other Castilian symbols; at the rear of this, the **Oratorium,** conserving a small *mihrab;* and the **Cuarto Dorado** («Golden Room»), entered from the **Patio del Mexuar.** This room was built under Mohammed V. The south front of the patio is one of the finest examples of Nasrite art. The Oratorium and the Cuarto Dorado both have balconies commanding magnificent views over the Albaicín.

The Palacio de Comares was organised around the **Patio de**

*Room of the Two Sisters.*

*Room of the Kings.*

**los Arrayanes,** or Patio de los Mirtos (Patio of the Myrtles), thus known because of the plants it contains, but also called the Patio of Comares, of La Alberca and of El Estanque. This is a wide, graceful courtyard whose fine-columned arcades, reflected in the water of the pool, confer on it a special beauty. Various rooms were lost from the south gallery of this patio when the Palace of Carlos V was built. The north arcade gives entry to the Sala de la Barca, or of the *Baraka* («blessing» in Arabic), antechamber to the **Salón de Embajadores** (Audience Chamber), which occupies the ground floor of the majestic **Comares Tower,** whose 45 metres make it the highest in the Alhambra.

The Salón de Embajadores is the most beautiful in the Alhambra. It is square with walls almost 20 metres high, but what most strikes the visitor is the refined beauty of its decoration,

*Moorish baths.*

carvings and plasterwork adorned with geometric and floral motifs as well as inscriptions from the Koran, and the vaulted ceiling, a masterpiece of Nasrite carpentry. The various balconies were, it seems, closed by stained-glass windows, the so-called *comarías* from which this palace and tower undoubtedly received their name. In this sumptuous room, where royal audiences were held, such historic acts as the surrender of Granada to the Catholic Monarchs and the signature by Ferdinand and Isabel and Christopher Columbus of the agreement by which the latter undertook the expedition which was to take him to America, also took place.

The **Patio de los Leones** forms the heart of the area reserved for family dependencies. A universally-famed image, the Lion Fountain bears an inscription posing the rhetorical question, «does not this garden offer a work whose beauty God de-

*Staircase to and upper section of the Rest Room.*

clared should have no equal?». The courtyard is surrounded by 124 fine white marble columns grouped in pairs except for those of the pavilions, one at either end.

On either side of the patio are different dependencies. The **Sala de los Mocárabes** communicates with the Patio de los Arrayanes, whilst the name of the **Sala de los Abencerrajes** recalls, it is said, the members of this family whose throats were slit here during the period of internecine strife in the kingdom, their heads piled up in the fountain in the middle of the room, the stains of its marble their blood. In the eastern section, the **Sala de los Reyes** is divided, in turn, into three compartments, each of which gives onto an alcove. These are decorated with 14th-century Italian-style paintings representing the ten Nasrite kings and romantic and courtly scenes. Finally, the **Sala de las Dos Hermanas** («Room of the Two Sisters»), whose name alludes to the two great slabs of marble

*Torre de las Damas in El Partal gardens.*

in the floor near the central fountain, formerly the chambers of the Sultana. This room opens up to two smaller rooms, that of Los Ajimeces and the **Mirador de Daraxa,** which commanded fine views until Charles V built his apartments just in front. At the foot of this oriel is the beautiful garden of Daraxa. From here, we can enter the **Patio de la Reja,** communicating with the **Sala de Reposo** (rest room) and the **Moorish Baths,** these last dating to the reign of Yusuf I and conserved almost exactly in their original form.

The garden of Daraxa leads to the **Jardines del Partal,** gardens which formerly contained the dwellings of the palace soldiers and servants. These terraces extend to the Church of Santa María, built in the 17th century on the site of the former mosque. At the entrance to the gardens is the **Torre de las Damas** («Tower of the Ladies»), which stands before a large. pool, with its five-arched loggia. To the left are three houses

*The Generalife: Patio de las Acequias and north portico.*

from the Moorish period which, though later modified, still retain their original structure. In one of these are interesting Moorish paintings, peculiar in that they ignore the Koran's prohibition of the representation of animals or human figures. Various towers form part of the wall around the site, many of them once converted into veritable little palaces.

On the adjoining Alhambra hill, known as El Cerro del Sol, stands the **Generalife,** summer residence of the Nasrite kings. Its most attractive feature are its splendid gardens in which water, as in all Moorish works, plays an important role. The building is arranged around the sumptuous **Patio de las Acequias,** through the centre of which runs a large channel fed by many spouts. Due to the successive alterations carried out since the time of the Catholic Monarchs, the Generalife is very much changed from its original shape, but nevertheless conserves intact its truly spectacular beauty.

Pedro de Machuca was commissioned with the construction of the **Palace of Carlos V** in 1526. This work was not completed, however, until the present century. The palace has a large courtyard measuring 30 metres in diameter with two floors colonnaded with Ionic columns on the lower and Doric on the upper. This is one of the finest examples of Spanish Renaissance architecture, though its position next to Moorish buildings is incongruous. Nevertheless, its construction affected only the royal cemetery and certain rooms in the Alhambra. Inside the palace are the **fine art and Spanish-Moslem art museums,** containing interesting works of Nasrite art.

The **Albaicín,** which we have been able to contemplate so many times from the Alhambra, is the old Moorish quarter and the original centre of the city. It still conserves its fundamentally Moorish layout, and a walk around its quiet streets reveals sites of singular beauty and interest. One of the entrances to

*Aerial view of the Palace of Charles V.*

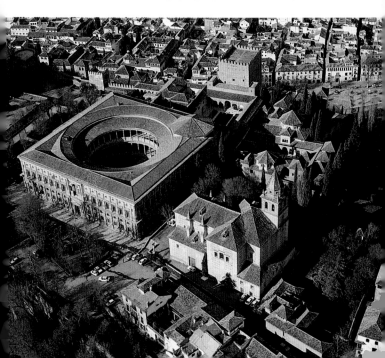

*The Albaicín, seen from the Alhambra.*

Granada, probably the main entrance, was the **Puerta de Elvira,** of which remains the gigantic exterior Moorish arch. The site on which the **High Church of San Salvador** now stands was formerly occupied by the main mosque of the Albaicín, of which only the Patio de los Limoneros (of the lemon trees) remains. The **Mirador de San Nicolás** is an excellent point from which to admire both the city and the Alhambra.

In **Carrera del Darro,** which starts in Plaza Nueva and stretches along the left bank of the Darro, begins one of the most pleasant walks in Granada. Here are such interesting buildings as the **Moorish Baths,** dating back to the 11th century, one of the oldest and best-conserved of Moorish Spain, and the Casa del Castril, a Renaissance palace with Plateresque front, now the seat of the **Archaeological Museum.** At the Bridge of Las Chirimías begins the Paseo de los Tristes («Walk of the

Sad Ones»), where funeral processions once passed. At the end of this passage are two paths, Camino del Rey Chico, leading to the Alhambra and the Generalife and of particular interest for the different views it offers of these Moorish palaces, and Camino del Avellano. The latter leads to the **Casa del Chapiz,** which houses the Granada School of Arabic Studies. The site is formed by two 15th-century houses and provides a good example of civil architecture after the Reconquest, mixing elements from different styles and cultures. This house marks the beginning of the **Camino del Sacromonte,** a path featuring cave dwellings carved into the rocks and ending at the Abbey of El Sacromonte, or Collegiate Church of San Cecilio, founded in the 17th century.

The cathedral and the Capilla Real are the most representative Christian buildings in Granada. The **Capilla Real** was ordered built by the Catholic Monarchs to house their burial places, though both died before it was finished and their mortal remains lay in the Convent of San Francisco de la Alhambra (now a *parador,* or state-run hotel) until they were transferred

*Front of the Lonja, or exchange.*

*«The surrender of Granada», by Moreno Carbonero.*

in 1521. The Capilla Real was designed by Enrique Egas and is a fine exponent of the Gothic Flamboyant style. Its entrance is in Calle Oficios, as the main doorway was integrated into the cathedral. The building has a Latin cross groundplan. The crossing is closed by a magnificent monumental grille, behind which are the royal tombs. The right-hand wall features a copy of Pradilla's painting of The *Surrender of Granada*.

The sepulchre was made in Genoa by the Italian artist Domenico Fancelli, whilst that of Juana, the Mad, and Philip, the Handsome, is the work of Bartolomé Ordóñez. Both are in Carrara marble. Below, steps lead down to the crypt containing the coffins of the four monarchs and Prince Michael, grandson of the Catholic Monarchs. Over the high altar is a fine altarpiece by Felipe Vigarny with, one either side, the praying figures of Ferdinand and Isabel, attributed to Diego de Siloé. Also interesting are the paintings, particularly the *Triptych of the Passion* by Dierick Bouts.

The entrance to the **Sacristy** is to the right of the tombs. In it is installed the Chapel Museum, containing various royal objects such as Isabel's crown and sceptre and the sword of King Ferdinand, as well as a good collection of Flemish and Italian painting, featuring masterpieces by Van de Weyden, Dierick Bouts and Hans Memling, Botticelli and Perugino.

The **cathedral** was built on the site of the main mosque by order of the Catholic Monarchs. It was designed in Gothic style by Enrique Egas and work began in 1521, to be continued in Renaissance style by Diego de Siloé in 1528. It was finally completed in 1704, when the cathedral was inaugurated. Various architects directed construction over this long period of construction, including, amongst others, Alonso Cano, author of the main front (1667), outstanding in its simplicity and originality. The tower of the front is unfinished and, as can be observed, one is lacking. Other fine doorways are the Puerta del Perdón and that of San Jerónimo, both by Siloé.

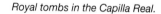

*Royal tombs in the Capilla Real.*

*The cathedral and the city.*

Granada Cathedral is considered one of the finest monuments of Spanish Renaissance art. Inside, the visitor is surprised by the dazzling luminosity of the building, an effect achieved by the studied play of light entering through the stained-glass windows and the dominant colours used (white and gilt). This high-columned cathedral has a nave and four aisles. The **Capilla Mayor** occupies an almost circular area 22 metres in diameter and at its highest point reaches a height of 45 metres. This architectural jewel is another masterpiece by Diego de Siloé. In white and gilt throughout, it is illuminated by 16th-century Flemish stained-glass windows. The paintings in the upper storey, by Alonso Cano, represent scenes from the life of the Virgin. The central tabernacle has a green marble base and is worked in silver. On either side of the nave are two colossal baroque organs and in the centre is a pantheon containing the tombs of Alonso Cano and Mariana Pineda. Of the various side chapels, those of Nuestra Señora de las Angustias and Nuestra Señora de la Antigua are the most interesting. In the latter there is a curious statue of Nuestra Señora de la Antigua, formerly the patron saint of Granada, brought here by the Catholic Monarchs after the fall of the city. The tower contains the cathedral museum, featuring important paintings and pieces including sculptures by Alonso Cano and Pedro de Mena.

Close to the cathedral is the **Alcaicería,** the former Moorish zoco and now a busy shopping area which still conserves its original character; **Plaza de la Bibarrambla,** formerly one of the nerve centres of the city; the **Corral del Carbón,** Moorish in origin and used as an inn and storehouse; and **La Madraza,** opposite the Capilla Real and now much reformed, but formerly the Moorish university founded by Yusuf I. Of Christian buildings, we can mention **La Cartuja** in the outskirts of the city, a monastery founded by Gonzalo Fernández de Córdoba, *El Gran Capitán,* with fine sacristy and *Sancta Sanctorum,* magnificent examples of the exuberant baroque style.

*Cathedral: Capilla Mayor.*

*Map of Granada province.*

## ENVIRONS OF GRANADA

The **Sierra Nevada** rises over the city of Granada, a mountain range containing the highest peaks in the entire Peninsula. Its three most spectacular summits are El Mulhacén (3,482 metres), El Veleta (3,398 metres) and La Alcazaba (3,366 metres), whilst the sierra stretches out to the south in more gently rolling hills. A road, one of the highest in Europe, reaching an altitude of 3,390 metres, ascends to El Veleta, also reached by cable car. The view from the peak is splendid: on the Mediterranean side is the region of Las Alpujarras, with its terraced foothills and variety of vegetation, whilst towards the Atlantic we can see the sharp mountain peaks, deep precipices and almost sheer slopes of the snowy mountains.

At the foot of El Veleta is the Sierra Nevada skiing resort, with 2,500 hectares of ski slopes. The residential area, Pradollano, lies at a height of 2,100 metres and is just 35 kilometres from Granada. In summer, the Sierra Nevada offers visitors the chance to practise such other sports as climbing, hiking, pony trekking and mountain biking.

Three roads lead to **Las Alpujarras**: the same one which took us up to El Veleta and which continues to Lanjarón, closed in winter; that which begins in Granada itself, the most practical; and the road from Guadix. The picturesque region of Las Alpujarras has remained almost unchanged since the time of Moorish domination due to the fact that it was of difficult accessibility until very recently. This is a mountain zone stretching from the Sierra Nevada down to the sea, scattered with splendid white villages which cling to the hillside, all of them full of charm: Lanjarón, Orjiva (the western capital of the region, conserving remains from the Nasrite period as well as a lovely 16th-century church containing an excellent carving by Martínez Montañés), Pampeneira (near to which is a Buddhist monastery), Bubión, Capileira, El Barranco Poqueira (with magnificent views), Trevélez, Cadiar, Yegen, Válor, Ugijar, Jorairatar, Murtas, Turón, and so on.

*Ski resort in the Sierra Nevada.*

*Trogolodyte district of Guadix.*

Inland, the city of **Guadix** is renowned, above all, for its troglodyte site with caves carved into the rocks, apparently inhabited since prehistoric times, with whitewashed walls facing the exterior. A cave museum recreates a dwelling, providing an insight into the life led by the inhabitants of this curious zone. To the rear of it is the old Moorish *alcazaba,* or citadel. Other points of interest include the cathedral, designed by Diego de Siloé, Plaza Mayor, a colonnaded square, and the Santiago and Santa Ana quarters, which still conserve their Moorish character. A road from Guadix leads to the **Castle of La Calahorra,** a well-preserved early-16th century construction. Returning to Guadix once more, we take the road to **Baza,** whose Moorish remains include the *alcazaba,* the city walls and the 10th-century baths, as well as the Jewish quarter. Also interesting is the Collegiate Church of La

Huéscar:
Plaza Mayor.

Orjiva: parish
church.

*Salobreña.*

Anunciación, a Gothic-Renaissance building by Siloé. And, further on, **Huéscar** features the Collegiate Church of La Encarnación (15th century).

The landscape now changes as the coast of Granada opens to the Mediterranean. This coastline forms part of the Costa del Sol and though some of its towns have been transformed by the tourist boom, others have retained their original air. Such is the case of **La Herradura,** surrounded by green, and **Salobreña,** a white village in the foothills dominated by a castle originally built by the Phoenicians and reformed by the Moors.

Motril is the most important town and port on the coast of Granada. It is now an important tourist resort and boasts fine beaches and various monuments, including the Collegiate Church of La Encarnación and the Sanctuary of Nuestra

*Almuñécar.*

Señora de la Cabeza, standing on the site of a Moorish palace on a small hill overlooking the sea.

**Almuñécar** has also grown into an important seaside resort abounding in hotels and holiday apartments. The origins of the town go back to ancient times, however, as are demonstrated by the Phoenician and Roman remains found here, including the aqueduct and the Torre del Monje. Its privileged situation made it the object of frequent attacks as well as the point of entry of various civilisations including the Moorish, as Abderramán I, founder of the Caliphate of Córdoba, is said to have landed here. The Castle of Alumuñécar was built over the foundations of a Moorish fortress by order of Emperor Charles V, and other attractions include the Archaeological Museum, installed in Roman galleries, and the Ornithological Gardens, featuring many species of exotic birds.

*Aerial view from the Gibralfaro hill: bullring and Paseo de la Farola.*

## MALAGA

Inhabited since ancient times, Málaga is the ideal city for visiting on foot. Its historic centre, containing the city's monumental treasures, stretches from the foot of Gibralfaro hill to the River Guadalmedina, but no visit to Málaga is complete without a tour of its port and pleasant gardens.

Since remote times, the **port** of Málaga has made it an important Mediterranean city. The present construction dates to the last century, the jetties and docks linked to the rest of the city by magnificent promenades. The most beautiful of these is, without a doubt, the **Paseo del Parque.** The park is characterised by its exuberant flora, mostly sub-tropical, in an area of over 30,000 m² dotted with various fountains and monuments to such illustrious personages as the Malagan

Partial view of Málaga from the Gibralfaro hill: the port, the Paseo del Parque and, in the foreground, the Puerta Oscura gardens.

«El Cenachero», in Plaza de la Marina.

**CENTRE OF MALAGA**

1. The cathedral
2. Archbishop's palace
3. Church of El Sagrario
4. Palacio de la Aduana
5. City Hall
6. Alcazaba and Archaeological Museum
7. Roman theatre
8. Gibralfaro Castle
9. Fine Art Museum
10. Church of Santiago
11. Picasso Foundation
12. Sanctuary of Nuestra Señora de la Victoria
13. Pasaje de Chinitas
14. Plaza de la Marina

TRINIDAD

PERCHEL

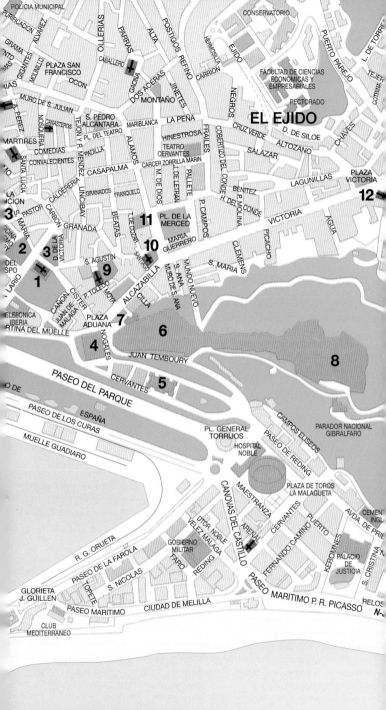

*Plaza de la Merced.*

politician Cánovas del Castillo. On the northern side of Paseo del Parque is the **Palacio de la Aduana,** an enormous square-shaped building, and the **City Hall,** a Renaissance construction which, in turn, adjoins the romantic gardens known here as the **Jardines de Puerta Oscura.**

On the way to Plaza de la Marina, we encounter the statue of *El Jazminero* and, in the square itself, the sculpture of *El Cenachero.* Further on stretches **La Alameda Principal,** a promenade opened in the early-18th century when this area was urbanised. This was the main avenue in Málaga before the construction of Paseo del Parque towards the end of the 18th century. Over the river are the Jardines de Picasso, a park containing a monument to the painter, one of Málaga's most famous sons, a bronze sculpture by Miguel Ortiz Berrocal.

Our tour of the historic centre begins in Plaza del Obispo. To one side of this is the Episcopal Palace, a building dating back to the 16th-18th centuries. The front which gives onto the square is the most beautiful and is presided over by a statue of the *Virgen de las Angustias.* The first floor contains the Diocesan Museum of Sacred Art, featuring various excellent items and paintings. In a small garden nearby is the **Church of El Sagrario,** built in the late-15th century on the site of the former main mosque, though of the original church on the fine Isabelline portal remains. Inside is a sumptuous 16th-century Mannerist altarpiece by Juan de Balmaseda.

Though the construction of the Church of El Sagrario was conceived in order to house the cathedral, this plan was soon abandoned and in 1527 a new project was drawn up which, despite work being interrupted on various occasions, brought into being by the 18th century the building we can now contemplate, though one tower was never finished, giving the cathedral its characteristic profile. Various master architects intervened in the work, most notably Diego de Siloé, to whom are attributed the original plans.

*Episcopal Palace.*

*The cathedral and the city.*

The main front, dating to the 18th century, stands on marble steps and features three elegant gates, the central adorned with a medallion depicting the Annunciation, those on either side displaying statues of the two patron saints of Málaga, Ciriac and Paula. The cathedral has a typically Gothic groundplan, though the style of the building can be considered as Renaissance. The principal features of the interior are the magnificent choirstalls, particularly the section by Pedro de Mena, the two identical organs with their over 4,000 pipes (late-18th century), paintings by Alonso Cano and, in the Chapel of Nuestra Señora de los Reyes, a statue of the Virgen de los Reyes donated by the Catholic Monarchs, and statues of Ferdinand and Isabel at prayer by Pedro de Mena.

On Gibralfaro hill stand the walls of the Moorish citadel or Alcazaba, residence of the Moorish governors of Málaga. This was built in the 11th century, during the reign of King Badis of the taifa of Granada. Its architecture is typical of Moorish fortresses: labyrinthine passages and numerous defensive towers giving access to the palace area. There were three palaces originally, only one of which, a Caliphal-style construction, has survived intact, the other two having been completely rebuilt in Nasrite style. The site is surrounded by leafy gardens and as we climb the hill the views over the city and the sea become more and more enchanting. Above the palace area, near to the keep, is a tiny Moorish quarter, considered one of the oldest of its type in Spain.

One of the Nasrite palaces now holds the city's Archaeological Museum, whose vast collections cover periods going back to prehistoric times. The Roman section features various heads, sculptures and mosaics, whilst there are also some interesting Visigoth items. The most extensive section, however, covers Moorish civilisation, most of the exhibits being from the Alcazaba. This collection features an important collection of Moorish ceramics, including various examples of gilt earthenware.

*Gardens and the Alcazaba.*

*Corner of a courtyard in the Alcazaba.*

At the top of the hill is Gibralfaro Castle, whose name comes from the Arabic for «mountain of the lighthouse» in allusion to the beacon which once stood here. The original fortress dates to the 8th century, but was rebuilt by King Yusuf I in the 14th century. This visit is particularly recommended as the hilltop commands the best views of to be had of Málaga and its bay. At the foot of the Alcazaba are the remains of a Roman theatre, which witnesses the importance of Málaga under the Empire. It was discovered in 1951 during restoration of the nearby Cultural Centre, and it appears that many stones, columns and other materials from it were used in the construction of the Alcazaba. It has recently begun to be used once more for performances of classical theatre.

From here, we can take Calle Alcazabilla to Plaza de la Merced to pay a visit to the **Picasso Foundation,** which occupies the house where the great painter was born. From here, a complementary route leads us to the end of Avenida de la Victoria, where we can visit the **Sanctuary of Nuestra Señora de la Victoria,** a church founded by Ferdinand the Catholic on the site of his encampment during the siege of Málaga. The church houses a magnificent statue of the Virgen by Pedro de Mena and a carving of the *Virgen de la Victoria* Málaga's patron saint of longest standing, but is best-known, nevertheless, for its impressive, awesomely solemn crypt and pantheon of the counts of Buenavista.

Returning to the city centre, we find the Fine Arts Museum (Museo de Bellas Artes) in Calle San Agustín, housed in the Palacio de los Condes de Buenavista. This is a 16th-century building combining Renaissance and Mudéjar elements. The museum's collections include works of the first order by

*Roman theatre.*

*Pasaje de Chinitas.*

Zurbarán, Murillo, Alonso Cano, José de Ribera, Benlliure, etc, as well as some early pieces by Picasso.

Close to this museum is the **Church of Santiago,** which features a fine Mudéjar tower, and the popular **Pasaje de Chinitas,** one of the most charming areas in the whole city. This is a labyrinth of narrow streets which was a popular meeting-point in the 19th century and which, today, is full of atmosphere and history. Together with **Calle del Marqués de Larios,** the veritable nerve centre of the city, this is one of the busiest points in Málaga. At the bottom of the latter street is a monument to the Marquis of Larios by the sculptor Mariano Belliure.

Regarding local festivities, various important traditional celebrations take place here. In summer, the **August Fair** is held to commemorate the conquest of Málaga by the Catholic Monarchs. During the festivities, the city centre and the fair site are enlivened by colourful processions of horsemen and richly-decorated carriages. On 28 December, the entire province celebrates the **Fiesta de los Verdiales** (a kind of olive), a tradition dating back to times immemorial. On this day, bands of «verdiales» meet to sing and dance, wearing the traditional costume, the most striking element of which are the hats of the men, tied with ribbons, flowers and mirrors.

During **Holy Week,** Málaga delivers itself to the emotion of the traditional solemn acts, including the freeing of a prisoner each Easter Wednesday, a custom followed since the times of Charles III. Among the different processions, some of the most important pasos, floats, are those of El Señor de los Gitanos, of El Cristo de la Buena Muerte and of La Esperanza Perchelera. On Good Friday, the Silent Procession takes place, an impressive event which takes place in complete darkness and to the sound only of the rhythmic beating of drums.

*Holy Week: María Santísima de las Penas.*

*Map of Málaga province.*

## THE PROVINCE OF MALAGA

The Costa del Sol is one of the favourite destinations of visitors to Andalusia. Protected from the north winds, its climate is proverbially benign, allowing the tourist season to last all the year round. The coastline offers an enormous variety of landscape, from villages conserving all their historic character to resorts densely populated by high-rise buildings, from broad beaches to half-hidden coves.

Just 14 kilometres to the west of Málaga, we come to the first resort, **Torremolinos.** This former fishing village is now one of the most characteristic and popular resorts on the Costa de Sol. Its urban expansion has been spectacular, but the fishing quarter of La Carihuela is still worth a visit. The main attraction of Torremolinos is, however, its beaches: La Carihuela, El Bajondillo, Playamar, Los Alamos, Montemar, etc, making up a total of over nine kilometres of wide beaches of fine sand. Moreover, the leisure and restaurant facilities in the town confirm it as one of the leading resorts on the Costa del Sol, being both extensive and varied.

Next, connected to Torremolinos, is Benalmádena-Costa, another locality which has grown rapidly thanks to the tourist boom. The town proper is inland, and still conserves its whitewashed, tidy physiognomy so typical of the villages of Andalusia. The town has an interesting Museum of Pre-Columbine Art and, on the coast, the Moorish Bil Bil Castle, as well as the ruins of three 16th-century lookout towers: Torre del Muelle, Torre Quebrada and Torre Bermeja.

One of the main attractions of **Fuengirola,** the next resort on the coast, besides its seven kilometres of beaches, is its sea front, or Paseo Marítimo, which runs parallel to the beach and makes up, with the surrounding pedestrian streets, an important shopping centre. The town's most representative monument is a castle dating back to Moorish times, though now much deteriorated.

A turn-off from the main road now takes us inland to the nearby village of Mijas. This is a typical Andalusian mountain village

*Torremolinos.*

Mijas.

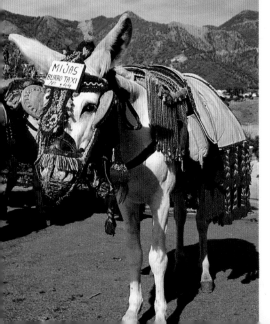

Donkey-taxi in Mijas.

*Fuengirola.*

which still conserves its traditional layout of narrow streets line by whitewashed houses with roofs of Moorish tile. At the topmost point of the village is a magnificent viewpoint over the coast. Mijas has a Miniature Museum with curiosities of all types, but perhaps its most peculiar attraction are its donkey-taxis offering tours of the village, even taking visitors to the hermitages of the surrounding area.

Marbella is one of the most emblematic resorts on the entire Costa del Sol, as well as being one of the most beautiful. Alongside the historic centre, the city has expanded over various periods. The Barrio Alto or San Francisco quarter grew up in the 18th century, whilst the Barrio Nuevo and Alameda quarters were urbanised during the 19th century due to the mining boom. In the 20th century, beginning in the 1960s, Marbella became a favourite tourist resort. «Old» Marbella still conserves its original layout of narrow streets and white houses which confer on the city a special charm. Plaza de los

*Marbella: Plaza de los Naranjos.*

Naranjos is in the city centre and contains the most representative monuments of Marbella: the City Hall (which occupies two buildings, one dating to the 16th century and the
other modern); the 16th-century Hermitage of Santiago; and
the Casa del Corregidor, also built in the 16th century and
boasting a beautiful Gothic-Mudéjar façade. The Municipal
Museum is installed in the old council building and contains
archaeological finds from all periods of the city's history to
works of contemporary art.
Other points of interest are the Moorish Alcazaba, the 16th-
century Hospital Bazán, now much reformed, and the Parish
Church of Nuestra Señora de la Encarnación, terminated in
the 18th century, as well as the pleasant Alameda Park, the
interesting Bonsai Museum and the various lookout towers
conserved on the coast. Around Marbella, the tourist boom

has led to the construction of many residential developments, many of them in neo-popular Andalusian style, adding to the attractions of the city.

Marbella offers the visitor a wide range of leisure activities, and also has three pleasure ports, one in the city itself, one at Cabo Pino, and Puerto Banús. **Puerto Banús** was built in 1970 and consists of a series of developments surrounding the port itself. It also has restaurants, luxury hotels and a huge diversity of shops. One of the main distractions here is to take a walk around the port, which is especially lively at night.

Some ten kilometres outside Marbella is **Ojén,** well worth a visit due to the splendid views it commands of the coastline and even, on clear days, of Africa. Continuing along the coast, the next port of call is **San Pedro de Alcántara,** a relatively new town (19th century) created when the Marquis of Duero set up an agricultural development here. It has a regular urban layout arranged around a main square containing the church

*Puerto Banús.*

*San Pedro de Alcántara: parish church.*

and town hall. Nowadays it is, however, an important tourist resort offering a wide range of activities. Nearby are the remains of a Roman villa and the ruins of the early Christian Basilica of Vega de Mar,

The history of **Estepona** goes back to remote times, but it is now an important tourist resort boasting over 20 kilometres of beaches. Of its Roman past the town conserves part of a Roman road and baths with ferruginous waters, whilst a number of towers bear witness to the Moorish settlement here, all of them restored in later years. Some 20 kilometres inland is Casares, a village with an attractive profile, situated on a hilltop. Its layout is typically Moorish and it stands out for the beautiful architecture of its white houses. Casares is the birthplace of Blas Infante, the ideologist of Andalusian nationalism. A monument commemorating its famous son stands in Plaza de la Iglesia.

**Ronda** is one of the most interesting cities in Andalusia. It stands on a magnificent site, crowning a rocky mount 750 metres in height, split into two by the famous Ronda Gorge which divides the city into two. On the south side is the old city, on the north the Mercadillo district and the new city. The old city corresponds to the Moorish *medina* whose physiognomy has been conserved. Here we can see the remains of the old Moorish city walls, now restored, and the two gates, those of Almocábar and of Carlos I. In Plaza de la Duquesa de Parcent, centre of the historic city, is the City Hall (16th century) and the Collegiate Church of Santa María la Mayor (16th-18th centuries), constructed on the site of a former mosque. Other interesting buildings include the palaces of Mondragón and the Marquis of Salvatierra and the Casa del Gigante.

The Puente Nuevo, a bridge joining the two halves of the city, is an impressive feat of engineering built between 1735 and 1793. It commands magnificent views over the gorge, reached by climbing down the Terraza del Campillo. Ronda's bullring is another outstanding symbol of the city. It is one of the most

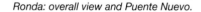

*Ronda: overall view and Puente Nuevo.*

*Antequera: «El Portichuelo» and the Church of Jesús*

important in Spain and is where the bullfighter Pedro Romero, to whom it is dedicated, developed so-called *toreo a pie* (bullfighting on foot). Other interesting sights in El Mercadillo district, adjoining the Puente Viejo, are the 14th-century Moorish baths.

Thanks to its rich history, **Antequera** is another important monumental city. Populated since ancient times, it flourished culturally and economically in the 16th century, when many of the palaces and churches we can visit today were built. The Municipal Museum, installed in the Palacio de Nájera, exhibits such treasures as the *Efebo de Antequera,* a collection of sacred art and interesting paintings. Some 12 kilometres from the city is El Torcal, a spectacular and surprising limestone landscape of strange and fantastic forms. Another recommended visit in the environs of Antequera is to the megalithic monuments of Menga, Viera and El Romeral, dolmens dating back to the Bronze Age and considered one of the most important such sites in Europe.

To the east of Málaga is La Axarquía, a region of varied landscapes, from coastal resorts to mountain villages, white-washed groups of houses conserving their Moorish origins. **Vélez-Málaga,** capital of the region, together with the adjoining **Torre del Mar,** is an important resort on the Costa del Sol, featuring such monuments as the Church of Santa María la Mayor, Mudéjar in style, and the Alcazaba, perched on the top of a hill. Adjoining it extends the San Sebastián district, the oldest in the city, a veritable labyrinth of tiny streets. Rincón de la Victoria has also been converted into an important resort thanks to the attraction of its splendid beaches. Nearby are some interesting prehistoric caves: El Higuerón, also known variously as the Cave of the Treasure, of the Spider and of Victory.

**Nerja** is another important locality in La Axarquía and the Costa del Sol which, though it has expanded greatly due to the tourist boom, still conserves its original 15th-century layout. The town boasts fine beaches and such interesting monu-

*Torre del Mar: sea front.*

*Nerja: Balcón de Europa.*

ments as the Church of El Salvador (17th century) and the Hermitage of Nuestra Señora de las Angustias (18th century), its dome adorned with frescoes by artists from Granada. Situated on the cliff-top, the viewpoint known as the Balcón de Europa commands panoramic views of the coast and mountains. There formerly stood here a tower and castle which were completely destroyed during the War of Independence. The famous «Balcony of Europe» now provides a splendid promenade leading to the city centre.

The **Caves of Nerja** are a leading attraction of this area. This is an immense grotto of enormous beauty, three of whose chambers stand out particularly: that of the Waterfall, that of the Cataclysm and that of the Phantoms. The second of these is the most spectacular, with a natural column over 30 metres in height and containing, like the others, many stalactites. Each summer, the cave becomes the incomparable setting for music and dance festivals, seating some 600 spectators. The upper galleries contain interesting cave paintings and there is also an Archaeological Museum exhibiting various objects discovered in the caves.

Inland, a short distance from Nerja, is **Frigiliana,** a town clinging to the hillside and one of the few localities whose original layout has remained unaltered. Throughout the town, ceramic plaques provide information about the history of Frigiliana through illustrations and explanations.

*Nerja: the caves.*

*Puerta de Tierra.*

## CADIZ

Considered the oldest living city in the West, Cádiz is thought to have been founded by Phoenician sailors in around the year 1100 BC. The *tacita de plata* - «little silver cup» - as the city is affectionately known, stands on a rock overlooking the waters of the Atlantic, joined to the mainland by a narrow isthmus, a peculiar emplacement which confers great beauty on it. Cádiz also enchants visitors thanks to its friendly inhabitants and its beautiful sights.

The main entrance to the old city is via the **Puerta de Tierra,** separating it from the modern city. This gate was opened in the city walls in the 17th century, nothing remaining of the Phoenician and Roman walls. Built between 1639 and 1751, this gate has a robust turret watched over by statues of Saint Servando and Saint Germán, patron saints of the city.

The route recommended to visitors continues along Cuesta de las Calesas, in which stands the 17th-century **Church of Santo Domingo,** in which is venerated a statue of the Virgin of the Rosary, patron saint of the city. At the end of this rise is the **Tobacco Factory** which housed the city corn exchange in the 17th and 18th centuries. Turning left, we come to the spacious **Plaza de San Juan de Dios,** nerve centre of the city. In this square is the **City Hall,** a finely-proportioned neo-classical construction whose clock chimes the hours to the tune of Fall's El Amor Brujo, and the **Arco del Pópulo.** The district of El Pópulo, the medieval heart of the city, extends between the City Hall and the New Cathedral and was reached by passing through three entrance gates: that of El Pópulo, that of La Rosa (to the left of the New Cathedral) and that of Los Blancos (in Calle San Juan de Dios).

The **New Cathedral** is the most important monument in

*New Cathedral.*

# Bahía de Cádiz

Punta Candelaria

PARQUE GENOVES

MUSEO DEL MAR

GOBIERNO MILITAR

**17**

CAMPO DE LAS BALAS

CASTILLO DE STA. CATALINA

HOTEL ATLANTICO

Playa de la Caleta

BALNEARIO DE LA PALMA

PUERTA DE LA CALETA

BALUARTE DE LOS MARTIRES

DRAGO MILENARIO

GRAN TEATRO FALLA

PLAZA FALLA

PLAZA FRAGELA

PLAZA MENTIDERO

PLAZA SAN ANTONIO

PLAZA DE MINA

IGLESIA SAN FRANCISCO

**14**

PL. SAN FRANCISCO

IGLESIA ROSAR

**15**

PLAZA DE LA OCA

OFICINA TURISMO

HOTEL FRANCIA Y PARIS

**13**

**10** **11**

**12**

**9**

**8**

PLAZA GASPAR DEL PINO

CENTRO CULTURAL

PLAZA GUERRA JIMENEZ

CORREO

PLAZ LIBER

IGLESIA S. LORENZO

SANTA LUCIA PONTE DENIL ROBLES

PLAZA CRUZ VERDE

IGLESIA LA PASTORA

PLAZUELA J. MACIAS RETE

PARQUE GENOVES

AVENIDA DUQUE DE NAJERA

JOSE PAREDES MONGE

JOSE CELESTINO MUTIS

CAMPO

AVENIDA

DOCTOR

GOMEZ

ULLA

PASEO DE CARLOS III

GONZALEZ TABLAS

PLAZA DE LOS COCHES

SIXTO FANO

SAN TELMO

HERCULES

CEBALLOS

SANTA ROSALIA

BENITO PEREZ GALDOS

FELIPE ABARZUZA

DOCTOR

MARAÑON

BOLIVIA

MATIA

GUATEMALA

CALLEJON DEL HOSPITAL

GRAVINA

SAN ISIDRO

ZORRILLA

GENERAL LUNA

VEA

BENDICION DE

DE

MURGUIA

DIOS

VEEDOR

NAVAS

ZARAGOZA

BENJUMEA

VIRGILI

SOLEDAD

CONCEPCION

DIEGO

ARIAS

JESUS NAZARENO

ENCARNACION

SAN

RAFAEL

BARQUILLA DE LOPE

BELEN

PASTORA

TIO LA TIZA

SAN JOSE

TORRE

PL. SAN FELIPE NERI

SANTA INES

SAGASTA

SACRAMENTO

SOLANO

HOSPITAL DE MUJERES

ARMENGUAL

MATEO DE ALBA

ROSA

MARIA

DE

ARTEAGA

CARDOSO

SAN VICENTE

CRUZ

BASQUIN

ROSARIO

CEPEDA

MARQUES DEL REAL TESORO

SAN MIGUEL

JAVIER DE BURG

JUAN DE DIOS

LONDRES

FERNANDEZ SHAW

S. FRANCISCO JAVIER

CADIZ

PORTERIA DE CAPUCHINOS

SAGASTA

SAN NICOLAS

PORLIER

VIRGEN DE LA PALMA

CONCEPCION

DE LA

VIDAL

TRINIDAD

JOVELLAR

CUESTA CAMPOS

COR. DE LOS CARROS

PROFESOR ALCINA QUESADA

DOCTORES MELENDEZ

CAPUCHINOS

SARGENTO DAPORTA

REGIMIENTO

DOMINGO MAC PHERSON

PICO ALBA

ANCHA

CANOVAS

SAN PEDRO

JUNQUERA

CERVANTES

VALVERDE

CASTIL

JO

NOVENA

MARINAS

PRESIDENTE RIVADAVIA

OBISPO CEREZO

PLATA

ENRIQUE DE LAS

FERNAN CABALLERO

ADOLFO

DE

CASTRO

BUENOS AIRES

ALAMEDA APODACA

GEN. MENACHO

SANTIAGO TERRY

AHUMADA

ISABEL LA CATOLICA

MANUEL

RANCES

ANTONIO LOPEZ

RAFAEL DE LA VIÑ

STO ESTO

FERMIN SALVOCHEA

PLAZA LOS POZOS DE LA NIEVES

PLAZA ARGÜELLES

HONDURAS

REP. DEL SAL

COSTA RICA

CONDE O'REILLY

AVEI

TINTE

CALDERON DE LA BARCA

ALAMEDA MARQUES DE COMILLAS

CARMEN

PLAZA LIBER

PERCON

PARAGUAY

ANGEL

SAN FELIX

VENEZUELA

LLURET

ARMCRUZ

DE

MACPHERSON

DEL

PLAT

MERC

CAMPILLO DE LOS COCHES

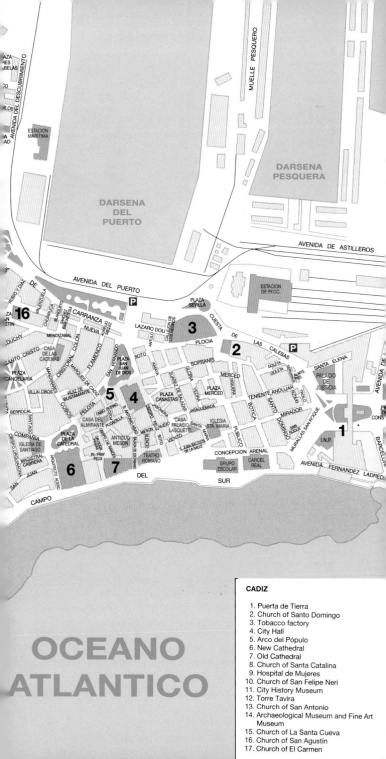

MUELLE PESQUERO

DARSENA
PESQUERA

DARSENA
DEL
PUERTO

ESTACION
MARITIMA

AVENIDA DEL DESCUBRIMIENTO

AVENIDA DE ASTILLEROS

AVENIDA DEL PUERTO

ESTACION
DE FF.CC.

PLAZA
SEVILLA

**16**

DE
VALENCIA
CHURRUCA
RUBIO Y DIAZ
ZA
N
STIN

CARRANZA

NUEVA

LAZARO DOU

**3**

PLOCIA

**2**

CUESTA
DE
LAS
CALESAS

SANTA ELENA
PALACIO
DE
JUSTICIA

MENDIZABAL
CASA
DE LAS
CADENAS
CRISTOBAL COLON
MARQUES DE CADIZ
FLAMENCO
SAN FERNANDO
PLAZA
SAN JUAN
DE DIOS
SOTO
ANCHA

SOPRANIS
MERCED
HIGUERA
GOLETA
GOLETA
SANTO
DOMINGO

SANTO
CRISTO
PLAZA
CANDELARIA
VILLALOBOS
BERROCAL
MANZANARES
RUIZ DE
BUSTAMANTE
COBOS
PELOTA
CASA DEL
ALMIRANTE

**5**

**4**

SAN ANTONIO ABAD
PLAZA
CANASTAS
PLAZA
MERCED
TEATRO
COMEDIA
TENIENTE ANDUJAR
BOTICA
MIRADOR
SAN ROQUE
MURALLAS SAN ROQUE

I.N.P.

**1**

P
DI
CONS

BARCELU

COMPAÑIA
IGLESIA DE
SANTIAGO
MAGISTRAL
CABRERA
PLAZA
DE LA
CATEDRAL
ANTIGUO
MESON
PL. FRAY
FELIX

**6**

**7**

CASA
PALACIO
LASQUETTI
IGLESIA
STA. MARIA
S. JUAN BAUTISTA
DE LA SALLE
VIENTO
TEATRO
ROMANO

CONCEPCION ARENAL
GRUPO
ESCOLAR
CARCEL
REAL

AVENIDA FERNANDEZ LADRE

CAMPO

DEL
SUR

# OCEANO
# ATLANTICO

## CADIZ

1. Puerta de Tierra
2. Church of Santo Domingo
3. Tobacco factory
4. City Hall
5. Arco del Pópulo
6. New Cathedral
7. Old Cathedral
8. Church of Santa Catalina
9. Hospital de Mujeres
10. Church of San Felipe Neri
11. City History Museum
12. Torre Tavira
13. Church of San Antonio
14. Archaeological Museum and Fine Art Museum
15. Church of La Santa Cueva
16. Church of San Agustín
17. Church of El Carmen

*Plaza del Tío de la Tiza.*

Cádiz. It was built between 1722 and 1853 in baroque and neo-classical style. Its interior features good cedar and mahogany choirstalls by Pedro Duque Cornejo and various paintings and carvings in the side chapels, but above all the crypt which contains the tomb of, amongst others, the great composer Manuel de Falla, a native of Cádiz. The **Cathedral Museum** contains excellent paintings and a magnificent collection of silverwork including the silver «Custodia del Corpus», a monstrance almost five metres in height weighing almost a tonne, the Flamboyant Gothic Monstrance of «El Cogollo» and that of «El Millón» (encrusted with thousands of precious stones).

Nearby is the **Old Cathedral,** or **Church of Santa Cruz.** This was built as a cathedral after the city as conquered from the Moors by Alphonse X, the Wise, in 1262, and was rebuilt in

1602 after being destroyed during the English siege. It contains good paintings and sculptures. Continuing along El Campo del Sur we come to the **Church of Santa Catalina,** containing works by Murillo, whilst to our right extends the district of La Viña, one of the most popular and oldest in the city, with such charming spots as Plaza del Tío de la Tiza, Calle Cardoso, Calle María Arteaga, etc. In Calle del Obispo Calvo y Valero is the former **Women's Hospital,** or Hospital of Nuestra Señora del Carmen, with a graceful staircase and El Greco's famous painting of The *Ecstasy of Saint Francis.* Close by, in Calle San José, is the **Oratorium of San Felipe Neri,** where commemorative plaques remind us that this was where the parliament of the Courts of Cádiz met during the French siege in 1812. This late-17th century church, elliptical in shape, houses a magnificent *Immaculate Conception* attributed to Murillo. Beside it, in Calle Santa Inés, is the **City History Museum,** containing a model of the city in wood and ivory corresponding to the year 1779. A little further on, in Calle Sacramento, we come to the **Torre Tavira,** an 18th-century

*Profile of the city featuring the towers of the Church of San Antonio.*

*Avenida Ramón de Carranza.*

tower used as a lookout post. This is the highest of all the towers which populate the roofs of the old city and it commands a charming and original view over Cádiz.

The **Church of San Antonio,** in the square of the same name, is distinguished by its baroque portal and twin pointed spires. From Plaza San Antonio, we take **Calle Ancha,** lined with noble mansion built from the second half of the 18th century onwards, when the city held the monopoly over trade with the Indies. In Plaza de la Mina is the **Archaeological and Fine Arts Museum,** one of the most interesting in the whole of Andalusia, with rooms dedicated to the works of Zurbarán which in themselves merit a visit to the city.

Taking Calle del Rosario, we find the **Church of La Santa Cueva,** containing paintings by Goya, and, further on, the **Church of San Agustín,** with carvings by Martínez Montañés.

From here, we can take Avenida Ramón de Carranza to begin a long seaside walk around the city. At the end of this first promenade, next to the pier, is the wide **Plaza de España,** in the centre of which is a monument to the Courts of Cádiz, which passed the 1812 Spanish Constitution, whilst on one side is the neo-classical seat of the Provincial Government. We now take the **Alameda de Apodaca y del Marqués de Comillas,** a lovely, typical promenade lined with trees and overlooking the sea. At El Baluarte de la Candelaria stands the Church of El Carmen, in baroque Colonial style. Next, we come to the **Parque Genovés,** a large, relaxing park.

Our visit now continues down to La Caleta beach. This tiny bay is protected at either end by the **Castle of Santa Catalina,** an austere late-16th century fortress and, on the left-hand side, that of **San Sebastián,** as well as the lighthouse of the same

*A nook in the Alameda del Marqués de Comillas, and the Church of El Carmen.*

*Cadiz has many fine beaches.*

name, standing at the end of the jetty. These constructions remind us of the time when the city was subject to attacks from Turkish pirates and English corsairs. **La Caleta beach** is the only one in the old city and is now one of the most popular. Here is the 19th-century spa hotel of La Palma. Cádiz also has other **beaches:** that of Santa María del Mar, not far from the Puerta de Tierra, small and pleasant, that of La Victoria, the largest in the city and one of the most popular, and that of La Cortadura, towards San Fernando, also very broad.

The most outstanding of the festivities of Cádiz is **Carnival,** spectacularly celebrated here. It generally takes place in the second week of February, 40 days before Easter. During Carnival, the city is one great theatre, the people donning fancy dress and the streets and houses adorned. Preparations for the festivities begin much before, however, as the different associations plan and prepare their contributions over the preceding year, producing satires on all types of news and events. It is even possible to attend the rehearsals in January. There exist four types of Carnival association: the *coro del Carnaval,* the *comparsa*, the *chirigota* and the *cuarteto*. A local saying has it that «the *coro* is the compliment, the *comparsa* the feeling, the *chirigota* the fun and the *cuarteto* the laughter of Carnival». The *coro* is made of around 30 people who ride in carriages. These choirs created a form of collective song, the *tanguillo de Cádiz,* accompanied by guitar and bandurria (a kind of lute). The *comparsa* has some 15 members and go around on foot, as does the *chirigota*, whose main instrument is the reed pipe, also used by the *cuarteto*, whose members also carry sticks which they knock together. Overall, Carnival - the words of the songs, the fancy dresses - sums up the peculiar character of the *Gaditano,* the native of Cádiz, capable, as the saying goes, of «laughing at their own shadow».

*The carnival in Cadiz.*

*Map of Cadiz province.*

## THE PROVINCE OF CADIZ

There is no location in Cádiz which does not merit a visit: from the villages of the Sierra with their whitewashed houses to the coastal resorts which, together with the coast of Huelva make up the Costa de la Luz, not forgetting the towns and villages of the fertile wine and bull routes.

Around Cádiz, closing the bay, are San Fernando, Puerto Real and El Puerto de Santa María making up a lovely route in which the singular landscape of the saltworks with market gardens and vineyards. The city of **San Fernando** acquired importance when Charles III made it the headquarters of the Maritime Department and it is now, after the reorganisation of the royal navy, the centre of the high command of the maritime zone of the Strait. Its monuments include the Castle of San

Romualdo, now much deteriorated, built to defend the port of Zuazo, originally a Roman construction separating the mainland from the Isle of León. The centre of San Fernando is arranged around Calle Real and features such buildings as the City Hall and the Teatro de las Cortes (scene of the first meetings of the Courts of Cádiz) and the baroque churches of San Pedro y San Pablo and of El Carmen, as well as the Church of San Francisco. Moreover, the Marine Observatory commands excellent views of the Bay of Cádiz.

**Puerto Real** owes its origins to the port founded by the Romans and rebuilt by the Catholic Monarchs in 1483. Its principal attractions are the 16th-century Church of San Sebastián and the Bosque de Las Canteras, a wood providing pleasant walks through pine trees to a hermitage.

**El Puerto de Santa María,** an ancient settlement, rose in importance after the discovery of America and is now one of the leading resorts on the Costa de la Luz, with an extensive offer of leisure facilities, hotels and restaurants. In Plaza de España is the Iglesia Mayor Prioral, or Church of Nuestra Señora de los Milagros, a 15th-century work containing the

*San Fernando: town hall.*

*Puerto de Santa María: Mayor Prioral Church.*

Chapel of La Virgen de los Milagros with a statue of the patron saint, and the Chapel of El Sagrario, with an altarpiece in Mexican silver. Other interesting buildings are the Castle of San Marcos, built in the 13th century on the foundations of an old mosque, and the bullring, in neo-Mudéjar style, one of the most important in Spain. Also worth a visit is the Rafael Alberti House Museum, installed in the house where the poet was born.

A city of strongly aromatic fragrances, **Jerez de la Frontera** is famed, above all, for its fine wines. The different varieties can be tasted at the local *bodegas,* wineries, one of the city's main attractions. Its monumental riches are concentrated, basically, in the city centre. Outstanding is the former Alcázar, an Almohade construction converted into the Chapel of Santa María la Real after the Christian reconquest in 1264. The cathedral, or Church of San Salvador, began to be built in the 13th century in Gothic style, but was not completed until 1750. It has a fine Churrigueresque front and contains paintings by Zurbarán. The Church of San Miguel, in Isabelline Gothic style with baroque front, contains carvings by Martínez Montañés, José de Arce and Roldán. The Church of San Dionisio, patron saint of Jerez, is a Mudéjar building dating to the 15th century. The city's civil buildings include the City Hall, with Plateresque front, the former Chapterhouse (Cabildo), now seat of the City Archaeological Museum, and a number of palatial noble houses. Jerez also has an unusual Clock Museum, «La Atalaya», as well as the important Royal Andalusian School of Equestrian Art, where visitors can admire the splendid equestrian ballet of classical and modern dressage.

In the environs of Jerez is the **Monastery of La Cartuja,** one of the foremost architectural monuments in the province of

*Jerez de la Frontera: wineries.*

*Arcos de la Frontera.*

Cádiz. Founded in 1477, the entire site is of outstanding beauty. The Wine Route, beginning in Jerez, continues with visits to Rota, Chipiona, Sanlúcar de Barrameda and Trebujena. The White Village Route begins in **Arcos de la Frontera,** one of the most beautiful villages in Spain. Arcos will delight the visitor due to its beautiful emplacement, perching on top of and extending along a gorge, and due to the Moorish air it still conserves, with its whitewashed houses and steep, narrow streets. The castle, restored on various occasions, was built by the Moors. The Church of Santa María, standing on the site of a Visigoth church and the remains of a mosque, was constructed after the Christian reconquest in 1264. The main portal is Gothic-Plateresque in style and the main features of the interior are the altarpiece and the treasure. The Gothic Church of San Pedro has a fine Plateresque altarpiece.

From Arcos, the White Village Route continues along the sierra north of Cádiz to Alcalá del Valle or east to Ubrique, crossing through the lovely Grazalema Nature Reserve. This route, taking us along picturesque roads, takes in a number of white villages, often perched on ridges and presided over by ancient castles.

**Medina Sidonia** is one of the main points on the Bull Route, which winds through the countryside of Cádiz, basically from Jerez to Algeciras, where the bull is a large protagonist on the landscape. Medina Sidonia conserves many fine monuments, including the ruins of the city walls and an old castle from Moorish times, the Ducal Palace and the Gothic Church of Santa María. Visitors will be delighted by a stroll around the medieval city with its steep, quiet streets.

It is still possible to find almost deserted beaches on the coast of Cádiz, particularly in the south. The winds on this coast are predominantly from the east, giving renown to such resorts as **Tarifa,** where an important windsurfing centre has grown up thanks to it. Tarifa is a lovely city surrounded by walls and

*Medina Sidonia: Plaza de España.*

*Algeciras: Plaza Alta and the Church of Nuestra Señora de la Palma.*

situated at the most southerly point of the continent of Europe, and was, with the nearby bay of Algeciras, where the invading Moorish armies disembarked in 711. This great bay contains three important localities: **Algeciras,** now one of Europe's most important ports, **San Roque,** where the people of Gibraltar settled when Spain granted England sovereignty over the rock, and **La Línea de la Concepción,** founded in 1730 when Philip V ordered the fortresses here built to defend Spain after the loss of Gibraltar. Inland from the coast of Cádiz, **Vejer de la Frontera** is a white village standing on a promontory.

La Línea de la Concepción.

Tarifa: Puerta Avenida Andalucía.

*The Alcazaba presides over the city.*

## ALMERIA

**Almeria** is a city of light, protected from the winds of the interior by a barrier of ochre-coloured mountains. Here, the waters of the Mediterranean acquire a deep blue tone. Since ancient times, Almeria has been an important seaport, the point of entry of different civilisations. The Moors gave it the name of *Al-miriya,* meaning «mirror of the sea», converting it into one of the key strongholds of Al-Andalus. According to a popular saying, «When Almeria was Almeria, Granada was just its farmstead». It was reconquered by the Christian armies in 1147, falling into Moorish hands once more ten years later, finally being taken by the Catholic Monarchs in 1489.

Our route begins in **Puerta Purchena,** nerve centre of Almeria and starting-point of its main thoroughfares. From Plaza

Manuel Pérez García we enter **Calle Tiendas,** since Moorish times the main centre of commercial activity in the city. Here is the **Church of Santiago,** a 16th-century building. On the corner with Calle Tenor Iribarne in the headquarters of the El Taranto group, are **Moorish aljibes** (cisterns) dating back to the 11th century, and at the end of Calle Tiendas we find the **Church of Las Claras,** an austere 18th-century monastery.

We now continue to **Plaza Vieja,** or Plaza de la Constitución. The former city centre is now one of the most peaceful and charming areas in Almeria, containing the **City Hall** and the monument to «Los Coloraos», dedicated the rebels against royal absolutism in 1831.

Passing through the arch adjoining the main entrance to the city hall and following Calle José María Acosta and Calle Almanzor, we come to the **Alcazaba.** Built on a small hill and surrounded by solid walls, this Moorish fortress dominates the

*Plaza Vieja. City Hall and monument to «Los Coloraos».*

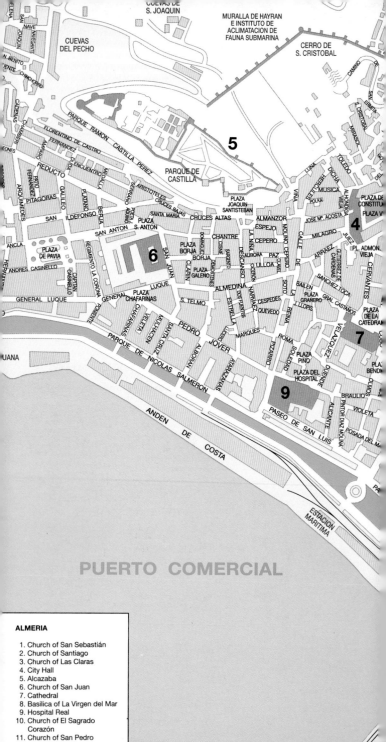

**ALMERIA**

1. Church of San Sebastián
2. Church of Santiago
3. Church of Las Claras
4. City Hall
5. Alcazaba
6. Church of San Juan
7. Cathedral
8. Basilica of La Virgen del Mar
9. Hospital Real
10. Church of El Sagrado Corazón
11. Church of San Pedro
12. Museum of Almeria

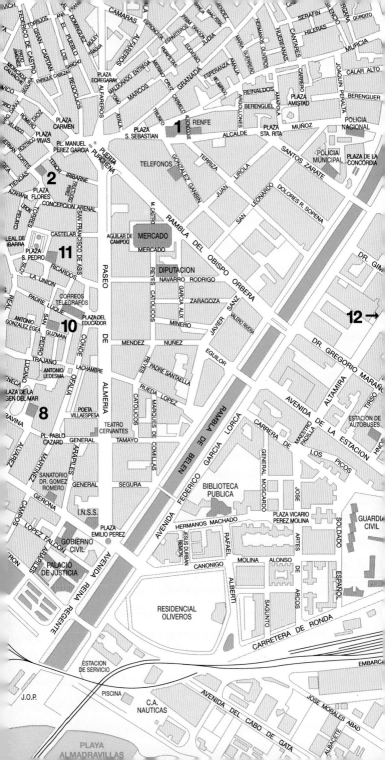

*La Chanca district stretches out at the foot of the Alcazaba.*

entire city. It was founded in the 10th century, during the reign of Abderramán III, and was later extended by Almanzor and by Hayran, first independent emir of Almería. The Alcazaba occupies an area of 43,000 m², divided into three terraced sections. The first, now completely gardened, was where the troops massed for expeditions and where the population took refuge in times of danger, whilst the second contains the ruins of the royal residence. The third section was rebuilt during the Christian era.

To visit the Alcazaba, we ascend steps and a zig-zagging ramp leading to the Puerta de la Justicia, next to which is the Torre de los Espejos, or Tower of the Mirrors, thus named because mirrors were used from this watchtower to signal news of any ships approaching the coast. We enter the second section by passing through the wall of the Torre de la

Vela, a tower whose bell rang out to warn the populace of any danger and which was also used to organise turns for irrigation. Of the small palace-city which formerly stood here, all that remain are part of the cisterns, the mosque, the baths for the troops and the dwellings of the royal servants. A reconstructed Moorish house gives us an idea of life in these times. Of the palace, only one wall remains, the Mirador de la Odalisca. A romantic legend tells of the love which grew up between one of the emir's favourites and a Christian prisoner: when they were found out, he threw himself to his death here, followed the next day by his lover, broken-hearted.

The third section includes the medieval castle built by the Christians after the reconquest. The entrance to this section leads us to the courtyard, in the centre of which is a deep well. At either end are towers. The keep, which served as a residence, is embellished with the arms of the Catholic Monarchs. The towers of La Noria and of La Pólvora command breathtaking views over the city and the sea, and of the wall which stretches from the Alcazaba to San Cristóbal hill, the **Institute of Climatisation,** a centre for the recovery of Saharan fauna,

*Walls of the Alcazaba and Cerro de San Cristóbal.*

*Cathedral: front and tower.*

and of **La Chanca district** with its picturesque houses carved into the hill.

At the foot of the Alcazaba, around Calle de la Almedina, the Jewish and Moorish quarters grew up after the reconquest. At the end of this street, the **Church of San Juan** occupies the site of the mosque, of which only the walls of the *quibla* and of the *mihrab* survive.

Returning to Calle de la Reina, where the inner walls separating the Almedina from the city formerly stood, we approach the **Cathedral,** which is surprising due to its fortress-like appearance, though it did, indeed, serve also to defend the population against continuous attacks from the sea. Construction began after the terrible earthquake of 1522, which destroyed much of the city and the port. Despite its external severity, the main portal is outstanding in its ornamental elegance. Inside is a fine Capilla Mayor, magnificent choirstalls by Juan de Orea and the tomb of Bishop Villalán, founder of the cathedral.

Not far from the cathedral is the **Basilica of La Virgen del Mar,** a 16th-century building devoted to the patron saint of Almeria. Taking Calle Real, formerly the main thoroughfare in the city, at whose end stood the Puerta de Mar, we reach the **Parque de Nicolás Salmerón:** where once stood warehouses pertaining to the port is now a pleasant park with arbours and pools. One of the most interesting buildings here is the **Hospital Real,** a fine neo-classical construction. In the opposite direction, after La Rambla de Belén, the sea front promenade begins, overlooking the beaches and the pleasure port. To return to our starting-point, the Puerta Purchena, we can now take Paseo de Almeria, a pleasant promenade along which 19th-century houses alternate with more modern buildings and shops. Much can be learnt about the city at the **Museum of Almeria,** whose archaeological collections include items from the paleolithic to the Spanish-Moorish periods. The museum also has rooms devoted to popular art and customs.

*Nicolás Salmerón park.*

*Map of Almeria province.*

## THE PROVINCE OF ALMERIA

This is the Spanish province which receives the most sunshine hours in the year, and whose skies are predominantly clear and cloudless. Protected from the north winds by the sierras of Enix, Alhamilla and Gata, the province enjoys a mild climate in winter and a hot climate in summer. Almeria is a province full of contrasts, moreover: from the fertile fruit and vegetable growing regions to the desert landscapes of **Tabernas** and surrounding area, where films set in the American West have often been made, filmsets now turned into tourist attractions with shows including falls from horses and saloon bar brawls. The coastline extending west of Almeria contains the most cosmopolitan and quickly-growing towns in the province. The broad, clean beaches, excellent leisure facilities and fine restaurants are the main tourist attractions. A pretty road winding along the rocky cliffs of the coast leads us, firstly, to **Aguadulce,** just ten kilometres from the capital, whilst another important tourist resort is **Roquetas de Mar,** whose fishing port still conserves a traditional air. Nearby is the Punta Entinas and Punta Sabinal Nature Reserve, the refuge of a variety of species of seabirds. **Almerimar** is a modern development with a splendid golf course, whilst the town of **Adra,** mainly devoted to farming and fishing, was founded by the Phoenicians and has a very different physiognomy from the more cosmopolitan places we have visited.

Some 15 kilometres inland from Adra is **Berja,** starting-point for a tour of the Alpujarra region of Almeria. Berja's most interesting site is its Plaza Mayor, containing the neo-classical buildings of the Town Hall, church and the Fountain of the Sixteen Spouts, whose waters come from the Sierra Nevada. La Alpujarra region contains a succession of tiny white villages of Moorish layout, giving it a particular charm. Back in the capital, near Gador is an important archaeological site, **Los Millares,** with a settlement and necropolis dating back to around 2700 BC.

*Aguadulce.*

*Adra.*

*Berja: Plaza Mayor and the «Fountain of the Sixteen Spouts».*

*Cabo de Gata lighthouse.*

On the eastern coast is the exquisite beauty of the **Cabo de Gata Nature Reserve,** which no visitor to the region should miss. Amidst this unforgettable landscape a steep, difficult road, but one which offers splendid views, leads to the Cabo de Gata lighthouse. This singularly wild area is characterised by sand-dunes, deserted coves and great rock formations. We now continue to **Nijar,** an authentic little village of white cube-shaped houses. Original artisanal activities are conserved here: the production of ceramics of Phoenician origin and of so-called jarapas, rugs made from different fabrics. Back on the coast once more, we come to **Carboneras,** a fishing village with a shingle beach, and **Mojácar,** one of the most typical villages in Almeria, Moorish in origin, a lovely, unique group of white houses huddled together on a hilltop. In the historic centre are the old castle and the church whilst, by the sea, Mojácar-Playa offers the visitor a variety of coves and beaches. The symbol of the *Indalo* is encountered throughout

Mojácar.

Sorbas.

*Vélez-Blanco.*

Mojácar. This is the sign of identity in Almeria province, besides having the magical power of freeing its possessors from all evil.

In an zone predominated by clay-red earth, we come to the hanging houses of **Sorbas,** clinging to the sides of a rocky hill and isolated by a gorge which acts as a natural divide. Sorbas is also famed for its red earthenware ceramics, employed particularly in the production of kitchen utensils.

To the north of the province is the old Marquisate of the Vélez family. The **Castle of Vélez-Blanco** is one of the loveliest in Spain, built by the first Marquis of Vélez between 1506 and 1515. The family died out in the late-19th century and the castle was taken over by a North American, who dismantled the Patio of Honour, which is now exhibited in the Metropolitan Museum, New York.

*Overall view of Jaén from the Hill of the Santa Catalina castle.*

## JAEN

Jaén lies amidst wild and beautiful scenery close to the Guadalbullón river. During the Moorish period, it was a resting-place for caravans *(geen),* from whence its name. After its reconquest by Ferdinand III, the Holy, in 1246, it became an important bridgehead for the conquest of the Nasrite kingdom of Granada. The splendour of the region during the 16th century has left its mark on Jaén, outstandingly in the case of the cathedral, one of its most important monuments and the starting-point for our tour of the city.

The **cathedral** began to be built in 1492, though it was not finally completed until 1802. It stands on the site of a mosque which was converted into a Christian church after the Reconquest. The original plans were drawn up by Pedro

López and Enrique Egeas, but the works took a new direction when Andrés de Vandelvira, creator of many monuments in both the city and province of Jaén, took over. The Renaissance style predominates in the cathedral, though the vaults and the main front are baroque. The majestic portal is flanked by twin towers and is decorated with great stone sculptures. Inside, worthy of special attention are the choirstalls and the Capilla Mayor, the latter containing the relic of «La Santa Faz», said to have been one of the cloths used by Veronica to clean the face of Christ. The reliquary is in pure gold encrusted with precious stones. Adjoining the cathedral are the Sacrary, designed by Ventura Rodríguez, and the Sacristy, by Vandelvira, whose crypt contains the Cathedral Museum.

Near to the cathedral, in Plaza de San Francisco, the former Franciscan convent is now the seat of the **Provincial Govern-**

*Main front of the cathedral.*

**15**

ZUMBAJARRA

CIRCUNVALACION

STA. BARBARA

HOSPITAL? MUJERES?

SANTISIMA TRINIDAD

EMPEDRADA

TRAV. PEÑUELAS

PRACTICANTE

SANTO DOM

LLANA DE SAN JUAN

PEÑUELAS

CONCEPCION VIEJA

**10**

PL. H. MUJERES

CARRETERA

DE

CEBOS RUIZ

MOLINOS

REVENTON

SAN BLAS

PALACIO VILLARDOMPARI

BRONERAS

CAP PALACIOS

DENAS

LA PAZ

ERVAS

BUENAVISTA

ALEGRIA

CLAVEL

SORIA DE

VICUARIO

PLAZA DE SAN JUAN

S ANDRES

**9**

**11**

HORNO

P. DE GRANADA

FUENTE NUEVA

PALACIO QUESADA

POZO

DUQUE

CAPITAN

ARANDA ALTA

CALVACHE

MAESTRO MACIAS

SANTIAGO

CRUZ VERDE

OTILITERO

ELVIN

ALCALA VENEGAS

AGUILAR

SAN ANTON

SAN PEDRO

MOLINA

ROSTRO

SANTA CRUZ

**5**

JESUS

ALMAGRO

SAN LORENZO

PARRILLA

PLAZA H. SANTIAGO

CIPRES

SEVILLANOS

ARROYO DE SAN

FUENTE DE LOS CAÑOS

FUEN ARRAB

HUE

MERCED ALTA

ALMENDROS

RUIZ GIMENEZ

LOS MACIAS

ANGELES

CAMPANAS

PALMAS

CORONADA

**7**

**8**

ARCO

LAS NOVIAS

MERCED BAJA

PLAZA DE LA MERCED

**6**

DIOS

AGUILAR

MARTINEZ

GRACIA

PLAZA CAÑOS

BAILEN

SANTA CLARA

OBISPO GONZALEZ

DUENDE

ARQUILLADA

MONTERO MOYA

COLEGIO

CASTILLO

CONSERVATORIO

CAMBIL

PLAZA SAN BARTOLOME

M. DE SAN AGUSTIN

HIGUERA

LAS HUERTAS

MILLAN DE PRIEGO

CARRERA DE JESUS

CERON

MADRE DE DIOS

PL. DE LA AUDIENCIA

COCHES

BAÑOS

ALDANA

HUERTA DE LA ROSA

**4**

SERRANO

PL. DE STA. MARIA

MAESTRA

LOPEZ BARAJAS

CERVANTES

CRUCES

M. DE SAN PRADO

PLAZA MORERAS

PLAZA AGUSTIN

CASTILA

MAESTRO

MARTINEZ

ALFONSO

CAMPANAS

LA PARRA

PLAZA CRUCES

RUIZ ROMERO

SALIDO

ASTORGA

CAP OVIEDO

ANGEL

ALMENA

ARCO DEL CONSUELO

**1**

SAGRARIO

PLAZA DE SAN FRANCISCO

CALLEJON DE LAS FLORES

PALACIO PROVINCIAL

PLAZA JARDINILLOS

PRINCIPE

JULIO

ABADES

PALACIO COVALEDA NICUESA

PALACIO DE LOS VELEZ

**2**

PL. DEL POSITO

ESPARTERIA

ARAZANAS

BERBESCOS

S CLEMENTE

F. MENDIZABAL

SOLEDAD TORRES ACOSTA

PLAZA

RILLA

HOGUERAS

RAMON Y CAJAL

PALACIO DE LOS VILCHES

LOS MOLINOS

IGLESIA SAN ANTONIO

BARRANCO

MUÑOZ

HURTADO

BERNABE

CRONISTA CAZABAN

PESCADERIA

ROLDAN Y MARIN

PASEO DE LA

OLID

MESA

MORALES

MACHIN

SORIANO

MURALLA DE BALEN

NUEVA

ANTON DE CUELLAR

CID

CAMPEADOR

REYES C

RIVERA

GARNICA

SAN FERNANDO

HURTADO

PLAZA DE LA CONSTITUCION

NAVAS DE TOLOSA

CORREA WEGLSON

PIO XII

PLAZA COCA LA PIÑ

MIGUEL

SALINEROS

LOS ROMEROS

IGNACIO FIGUEROA

CUATRO TORRES

GRACIANS

ZUBELZU

VIRGEN DE LA CAPILLA

**3**

PEDRO DIAZ

ARANDA

TEODORO

CHINCHILLA

CALVACHE

LUZADERAS

CUESTA BELEN

ANGUITA ROLDAN

ADAR

VENTE MONTILLO

COBO MEDINA

DR. SAGAZ

SALSIPUEDES

VERGARA

PASEO DE LA HARINA

PLAZA BELEN

ALCEJOS

LAS BERNARDAS

P. DE SAN GENOVEVO

LABRADORES

SANTA CATALINA

ER

ARTESANOS

ADARVES BAJOS

PUERTA DEL ANGEL

GENERAL CASTAÑOS

SAN JOSE

JUAN RINCON

TRES MORILLAS

AIRE

GUADALQ

CONVENTO BERNARDAS

CAMARA

PLAZA DE TOROS

ALAMEDA

CAMINO DE LAS CRUCES

BRETAÑ

FERIAL DE FELIPE ARCHE

**JAEN**

1. The cathedral
2. Provincial government
3. Church of San Ildefonso
4. Convent of Las Carmelitas Descalzas
5. Church of La Merced
6. Arco de San Lorenzo
7. Church of San Bartolomé
8. Convent of Santa Clara
9. Church of San Andrés
10. Church of San Juan
11. Moorish baths
12. Monastery of Santo Domingo
13. Church of La Magdalena
14. Provincial Museum
15. Castle of Santa Catalina

*Plaza de la Constitución.*

**ment.** This building has a fine inner courtyard. Taking Calle Hurtado, we come to the **Church of San Ildefonso,** a Gothic building with Renaissance tower containing the statue of the Virgen de la Capilla, patron saint of the city. Returning to the cathedral , we take Calle Maestra, at the end of which is the **Arch of San Lorenzo** (15th century). **Plaza San Bartolomé** contains the church of the same name, with Gothic baptismal font, fine Mudéjar coffering and a sculpture attributed to Montañés.

On our way to the **Church of La Magdalena,** the oldest in Jaén, we pass through the areas of the city which have best retained their original Oriental air. These narrow streets reveal mansions and churches which are in sharp contrast to the whitewashed houses with their ochre-coloured roofs. We can mention just a few of the monuments of interest here. The **Church of San Andrés** was built on the site of a synagogue in Mudéjar style though with elements reminiscent of Hebrew architecture. Inside, the Santa Capilla has a magnificent grille by the maestro Bartolomé. The Palacio de Villardompardo houses the **Moorish Baths,** recently restored. These date to the 11th century and cover an area of 600 m². The main front and cloister of the **Convent of Santo Domingo** are by Vandelmira. Now the seat of the City Archives, this building formerly housed the old university.

At the top of the hill is the **Castle of Santa Catalina,** now converted into a *Parador,* or state-run hotel. It was built in the 13th century by the Nasrite king Alhamar and reconstructed by Ferdinand III. This is a splendid edifice of cubic forms featuring a fine keep, various towers, parade ground and the Chapel of Santa Catalina. The castle dominates the entire city, offering excellent views of the Sierra Morena.

Near to Plaza de las Batallas, in Paseo de la Estación, is the **Provincial Museum.** The building itself contains the Portal of San Miguel, recovered from the church of the same name, now lost. The rooms devoted to archaeological finds feature such valuable exhibits as the Iberian bull of Porcuna and an early Christian sarcophagus from Martos.

*Santa Catalina castle.*

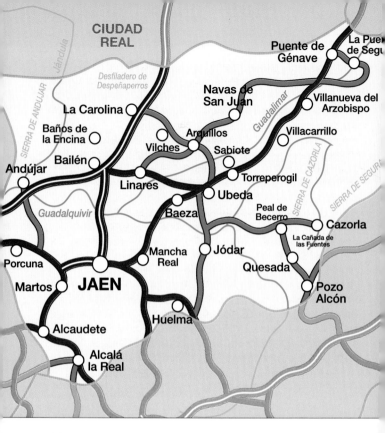

*Map of Jaén province.*

## THE PROVINCE OF JAEN

The province of Jaén is distinguished by its wide, reddish-coloured fields of olive trees. Not in vain is it Spain's biggest producer of olives, both for eating and for the production of oil. But Jaén province also offers a variety of landscapes and contains important monumental cities such as Ubeda and Baeza, veritable jewels of Spanish Renaissance architecture. The monumental city of **Baeza** contains works from various artistic periods, though most of its important buildings date to the 16th and 17th centuries. Particularly charming is Plaza de los Leones, an emblem of the city. This square contains the fountain which gives it its name, with the Iberian-Roman female figure from Cástulo; the former 16th-century slaughterhouse (carnicería), featuring an enormous coat of arms of Charles V; the 16th-century Casa del Pópulo with a fine Plateresque-Renaissance front; and, adjoining this last, the

Puerta de Jaén, formerly part of the city walls; and the Arch of Villalar. Walking around the surrounding streets reveals to us a multitude of charming sights and beautiful monuments. In the words of Antonio Machado, the great poet who taught French in this city, «Baeza, I will dream of you when I no longer see you». Particularly interesting are the buildings of the old university (16th century), the Church of Santa Cruz (Romanesque, with Gothic chapel), the Palace of Jabalquinto (with excellent Flamboyant front), the cathedral (with examples of Mudéjar, Gothic, Renaissance and baroque art), opposite which are the *Casas Consistoriales Altas,* the former *Alhóndiga* (corn exchange), the City Hall (Plateresque, formerly the Palace of Justice and Prison) and the Church of El Salvador (a mixture of the Romanesque, the Gothic and the Renaissance styles).

Its magnificent monuments have made **Ubeda** known as the «Salamanca of Andalusia». Its monumental riches are certainly impressive, even more so than Baeza. In Plaza Vázquez de Molina is the most typical building in the city, a masterpiece of Spanish Renaissance art: The Sacred Chapel of El Salva-

*Baeza: Plaza de los Leones.*

*Ubeda: Sacred Chapel of El Salvador.*

dor. Designed by Diego de Siloé, it was completed by the principal artifice of the building, Andrés de Vandelvira. This square is completed by a number of other magnificent buildings: the *Parador,* installed in a 16th-century palace, the former *Pósito,* the Palace of the Marquis of Manceras and the Palace of Las Cadenas, the Church of Santa María de los Reales Alcázares (built between the 12th and 15th centuries) and the Cárcel del Obispo, a monastery. Other beautiful examples of Spanish Renaissance art are the churches of San Pablo and San Nicolás, the Hospital of Santiago (by Vandelvira) and a number of fine palaces. The Royal Monastery of Santa Clara is the oldest in Ubeda and contains elements of Romanesque and Renaissance art, as does the nearby Church of San Pedro. The City Archaeological Museum is installed in the Casa Mudéjar.

The environs of the city provide a fine opportunity to follow the popular saying and «lose ourselves in the hills of Ubeda», an

*Torreperogil.*

*Walls of Sabiote castle.*

*Cazorla.*

expression which dates from the time of Ferdinand III, during the siege of the city. It seems that one of the king's knights was unable to play a part in the conquest because, as the noble himself explained, he had become lost in the hills on the way to Ubeda. The countryside contains two interesting towns: **Torreperogil** and **Periote.** The former features the singular Torres Oscuras (13th century), dark towers giving the town its name. The walls and castle of Sabiote, Moorish in origin, were built on Roman foundations. The solid castle now presents a Renaissance aspect, however, due to the reforms carried out in the 16th century. Another interesting sight here is the Church of San Pedro, featuring a fine Renaissance front.

To the east extends the **Nature Reserve of the Sierras of Cazorla and Segura,** along with that of Doñana the largest in Andalusia. The park, with an area of over 200,000 hectares, is a veritable oasis of extraordinarily beautiful forests. It also contains a hunting reserve in which birds of prey, deer and boar predominate. The almost-mythical Guadalquivir river is born in La Cañada de las Fuentes in the Sierra de Cazorla, at an altitude of 1,400 metres. Taking any of the surrounding towns as the starting-point, excursions on foot, on horseback or by car can be made, and guides are also available.

**Cazorla** is the principal town in the area. Its white houses extend amongst the foothills of the Sierra with, at the top, the Moorish Castle of La Yedra. This spot commands excellent views and also contains an Ethnographic Museum. The ruins of the old castle, also known as the «Castle of the Five Corners», stand in an eminent position. The historic town, with steep, narrow streets, also contains the interesting Plateresque Church of Santa María, designed by Vandelvira.

**Quesada** still conserves its medieval walls and the ruins of a castle. Like almost all the towns of the region, it is characterised by its white houses, amongst which stand various Renaissance buildings, principally the parish church. Also interesting is the museum dedicated to the great painter Rafael Zabaleta, born in Quesada. Near the town, prehistoric caves with paintings have been discovered, and also worth a visit is

*Quesada.*

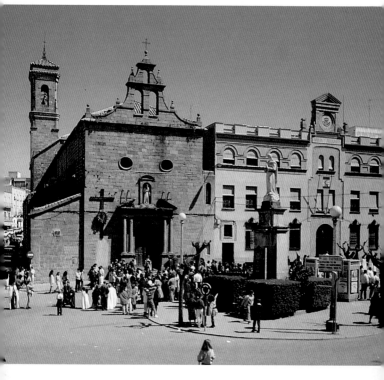

*Linares: Plaza Mayor.*

the Sanctuary of Tíscar at the foot of the peak known as the Peña Negra, to which a *romería* (religious procession) takes place every year on the first Sunday in September.

In the northwest of the province is a zone known as the «region of mines and battles». Of battles because the troops of Napoleon suffered a famous defeat at **Bailén** in 1808, a defeat which signalled the beginning of the end of their occupation of Spain, whilst in 1212 a battle took place on the plains of **Navas de Tolosa** which opened the way for the Christian reconquest of Andalusia from the Moors. Not in vain is the Despeñaperros Pass often known as the «Gateway to Andalusia», for to control it is to command access to the entire region.

**Linares** is an important industrial and mining town containing such sights as the Church of Santa María la Mayor and the Church of San Francisco, Plaza Mayor, the palaces of Zambrana and Los Orozco, and the Town Hall. The local Archaeological

Museum is housed in the Torreón building, and its exhibits feature findings from the Roman city of Cástulo, a 3rd-century BC settlement some six kilometres outside Linares. A visit to Cástulo should also take in the Piélago bridge, also built by the Romans in the 3rd century BC. The Linares bullring is dedicated to Manolete, as it was here that he was gored to death by the bull Islero in August 1947.

Of its Moorish origins, the olive-growing town of **Andújar** conserves the 11th-century walls. The monuments here include the Romanesque and Gothic Church of Santa María la Mayor, with fine belltower («Torre del Reloj») and portal. Inside is a painting by El Greco. The Church of San Miguel has a good wrought iron grille. The Palacio Municipal was formerly used as the local theatre. Also interesting are the Palace of Los Niños de Don Gome and the Palace of Justice, both built in the 15th century. To the north, in the heart of the Sierra Morena, the Nature Reserve of the Sierra de Andújar is a splendid attraction for visitors. Worth a visit here is the **Sanctuary of the Virgen de la Cabeza,** built in the 15th century and the object of a *romería* which takes place each year at the end of April.

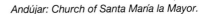

*Andújar: Church of Santa María la Mayor.*

*Cathedral of La Merced.*

## HUELVA

Situated on the banks of the Atlantic, at the meeting-point of the Tinto and Odiel rivers, Huelva is a peaceful provincial capital which is well worth a visit. The city's origins are remote, but it conserves few vestiges of its history as an earthquake in 1755 destroyed it almost completely.

Our tour of Huelva begins in Plaza de la Merced, where the church of the same name stands, converted into **cathedral** in 1953 after the creation of the dioceses of Huelva. The Convent of La Merced was founded in the early-17th century, and was a barracks and a hospital before being converted into a cathedral. The 18th-century front, reddish in colour, is reminiscent of the Colonial style. Inside is a 12th-century statue of Christ and a statue of the Virgen de la Cinta, patron saint of Huelva, by Martínez Montañés.

The **Church of San Pedro,** in the square of the same name, is the oldest remaining church in the city. It was built between the 15th and 16th centuries on the site of a Moorish mosque, and still conserves Mudéjar elements, though it was later reformed in accordance with baroque tastes, particularly the belltower. Next, we come to the **Church of La Concepción,** built in the 16th century and reconstructed after the 1755 earthquake. This church contains an interesting altarpiece and good choirstalls.

Nearby is the **Plaza de las Monjas,** the most charming and popular sites in the city. The pedestrian streets of this central zone have been converted into an open-air sculpture museum featuring works by various local artists. Next, we take Gran Vía, also known as Avenida Martín Alonso Pinzón, lined with such official buildings as the seat of the Civil Government, the City Hall and the Provincial Government headquarters. At the end of Gran Vía is the Casa de Colón (House of Columbus), a 19th-century building which has now been restored and converted into a cultural centre.

*Church of San Pedro.*

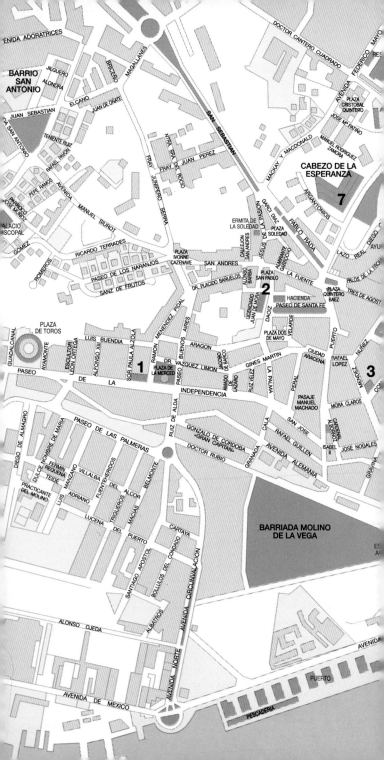

**6**

**5**

AVENIDA DE CADIZ

ALAMEDA DE SUNDHEIM

LUIS BRAILLE

AVENIDA E. MISS WHITNEY

RQUE DE LA
SPERANZA

PLAZA
DEL PUNTO

PADRE
ARCHENA

PINZON

AVENIDA

SOR ANGELA DE
LA CRUZ FERNANDEZ

NIÑA

PLAZA ISABEL
LA CATOLICA

BERDIGON

SAN CRISTOBAL

PADRE ANDIVIA

SANTA MARIA

PINTA

ITALIA

ALFONSO XII

MIGUEL

LA PAZ

REDONDO

RABIDA

GRAN
TEATRO

LOPEZ

MURILLO

SEVILLA

RICO

ITALIA

RAMON LOPEZ GARCIA

LUIS DE
VARGAS

CASTILLA

SANCHEZ BARCAIZTEGUI

CORREOS

LA VICTORIA

PEÑORISA

AVENIDA

ALCALDE
JOSE Mª AMO

LUCA DE TENA

IDALERAS

AVENIDA TOMAS DOMINGUEZ ORTIZ

AVENIDA DEL SUR

CADIZ

SANTO DOMINGO
DE LA CALZADA

A DOCE
CTUBRE

SAN LUCAR DE BARRAMEDA

JARDINES
DEL MUELLE

PLAZA
MARINA

HISPANOAMERICA

COMANDANCIA
DE MARINA

DE

NTE

ESTACION F.C.
DE SEVILLA

RECINTO
COLOMBINO

AVENIDA DE FRANCISCO MONTENEGRO

MONUMENTO A COLON
MUELLE DEL TINTO

ENIDA TRAFICO PES

# RIO ODIEL

## HUELVA

1. Cathedral of La Merced
2. Church of San Pedro
3. Church of La Concepción
4. Plaza de las Monjas
5. House of Colombus
6. Provincial Museum
7. Alonso Sánchez Park

*Bullring.*

The **Provincial Museum** is found in the Alameda Sundheim. Its collections are divided into three sections, one dedicated to archaeology, one to fine art and a third to the painter Daniel Vázquez Díaz, born in nearby Nerva and the author of the mural paintings on the discovery of America in the Monastery of La Rábida.

Huelva also boasts various pleasant parks and gardens, including the **Jardines del Muelle** and the recently-opened **Parque Alonso Sánchez,** a park of modern design commanding views over the entire city.

Standing on the top of a small hill some two kilometres from the city centre, past the Parque Moret, is the **Sanctuary of the Virgen de la Cinta,** whose splendid emplacement offers the visitor panoramic views ranging over the Sierra, the sea, the city and the river. Each 8 September, festivity of the patron saint of Huelva, a *romería* of long-standing tradition takes place at this white church of austere simplicity. Inside the building is a lovely carving of the Virgen de la Cinta and tiles commemorating Columbus' visit to the sanctuary.

In the opposite direction, at the confluence of the Tinto and Odiel rivers, some five kilometres from the centre, stands a colossal **monument to Columbus,** a stone sculpture by the North American artist Gertrudis V. Whitney, commemorating the great feat of the discovery of America, for Columbus started out on his epic journey from here. The history of Huelva is intimately linked with the discovery of America, as we can see by following the «Columbus Route» described in the following section of this guide. Huelva celebrates the discovery each August in the Columbine Festivities, during which bullfights, competitions and dances take place.

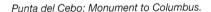

*Punta del Cebo: Monument to Columbus.*

*Map of Huelva province.*

## ENVIRONS OF HUELVA

Although Huelva has been considered a place of transit since its origins, the province contains a number of places of interest. To the north is the Sierra, in whose mounts nestles the village of **Aracena,** famed due to the Cave of Las Maravillas, one of the longest underground grottoes in the world. On the coast, known as the **Costa de la Luz,** traditional fishing villages have been converted into popular tourist resorts thanks to the attraction of their splendid beaches. Nevertheless, Huelva is associated, above all, with Christopher Columbus and the discovery of America. The so-called Columbine route takes in Moguer, Palos de la Frontera and the Monastery of La Rábida.

The **Monastery of La Rábida,** a 14th-century Gothic-Mudéjar monument, is where Columbus stayed before departing for the New World. It is here that he drew up the plans for his voyage and explained his theories to the prior and monks, who

*Monastery of La Rábida.*

*Murals by Vázquez Díaz in the Monastery of La Rábida.*

*Palos de la Frontera, with «La Fontanilla» in the foreground.*

supported his project. In the Sala de los Frescos, the mural paintings of Vázquez Díaz commemorate the discovery of America. Columbus and the Pinzón brothers set sail from **Palos de la Frontera** on 3 August 1492, heading for the Indies in their three famous caravels, returning here after their epic voyage of discovery on 15 March 1493. The Mudéjar door of the Church of San Jorge commemorates this historic episode, whilst the three ships were supplied with water before they set out from the «Fontanilla», a Mudéjar fountain with Roman curb. And in the Church of Santa Clara, a convent founded in the 14th century in **Moguer,** Columbus passed the night in prayer on his return from America in 1493, thus complying with the votive promise he had made on the high seas when his ship La Niña was in danger of being lost during a storm. The poet Juan Ramón Jiménez, author of «Platero and I» and winner of the Nobel Prize for Literature, was born in Moguer and is commemorated in various nooks of the city. An important

*A view of the Romería del Rocío.*

*Sanctuary of the Virgen del Rocío in Almonte.*

*Gibraleón: Church of Santiago.*

museum is also dedicated to the writer, and the house where he was born can also be visited.

Not far from Moguer is **Almonte,** where the popular *romería del Rocío* culminates (see the section on Seville). From here to an area covering part of the neighbouring province of Seville stretches the **Doñana National Park,** a nature reserve and wintering-place for many species of bird. The best time to visit this park is in autumn and winter, when migratory birds flock here and the marshlands are covered in water, composing a scene of exceptional beauty.

Other interesting sights near the capital include **Gibraleón,** a lovely village with Moorish fortress on the banks of the Odiel, and **Niebla,** which forms part of the «Wine Route», covering the Condado area. Niebla is surrounded by walls built by the Moors in the 12th century and in which various towers and five gates are conserved. The Alcázar, or Castle of Los Guzmanes, is also Moorish in origin, whilst the Roman bridge is one of the best conserved in Spain. Just one kilometre from Niebla is El Soto dolmen, an important prehistoric monument featuring many cave paintings.

*Niebla: Church of San Martín and Moorish arch.*

*Doñana national park.*

CIUDAD REAL

tollano

Villanueva de los Infantes

Valdepeñas

Alcaraz

ALBACETE

Puente de Génave

La Puerta de Segura

C-3210

Navas de San Juan

Villanueva del Arzobispo

La Carolina

Villacarrillo

Baños de la Encina

Arquillos

Vilches

Sabiote

Bailén

N-322

Torreperogil

Puebla de Don Fadrique

MURCIA

Caravaca de la Cruz

Andújar

Linares

Ubeda

Peal de Becerro

Cazorla

Huéscar

Vélez-Blanco

Porcuna

Baeza

C-328

La Cañada de las Fuentes

N-324

Jódar

Quesada

C-330

Vélez-Rubio

ance

Mancha Real

Martos

JAEN

Pozo Alcón

C-323

Cúllar-Baza

N-432

Alcaudete

Huelma

Baza

Huércal-Overa

Cuevas del Almanzora

C-336

Alcalá la Real

Guadahortuna

N-336

Caniles

Almanzora

Santa Bárbara

ora

Priego de Córdoba

Cantoria

Vera

ena

Montefrío

Purullena

Guadix

N-324

Sorbas

Turre

Garruch

Mójacar

Loja

GRANADA

Tabernas

Carboneras

Moraleda de Zafayona

Alcolea

Alhama de Almería

Nijar

Alhama de Granada

Agrón

N-323

Lanjarón

Orjiva

SIERRA NEVADA

C-332

Berja

Gádor

Rioja

SIERRA ALHAMILLA

ALMERÍA

SIERRA DE GATA

Axarquía

Vélez-Málaga

Frigiliana

Almuñecar

C-333

Motril

El Ejido

E-15

Aguadulce

Torre del Mar

Nerja

La Herradura

Salobreña

La Rábita

Adra

Roquetas de Mar

El Cabo de Gata

LAGA

olinos

ena

COSTA DE ALMERÍA

DEL SOL

MAR MEDITERRANEO

# CONTENTS

INTRODUCTION AND HOW TO USE THIS
   GUIDEBOOK ................................................................2

SEVILLE, HISTORIC CENTRE .............................................4
SEVILLE, FESTIVALS ...........................................................18
SEVILLE, EXCURSIONS .......................................................22

CÓRDOBA, CITY ....................................................................28
CÓRDOBA, EXCURSIONS ....................................................50

GRANADA, CITY .....................................................................52
GRANADA, EXCURSIONS ....................................................70

MÁLAGA, CITY ........................................................................76
MÁLAGA, EXCURSIONS ......................................................88

CÁDIZ, CITY ...........................................................................100
CÁDIZ, EXCURSIONS ...........................................................110

ALMERÍA, CITY ......................................................................118
ALMERÍA, EXCURSIONS ......................................................126

JAÉN, CITY .............................................................................132
JAÉN, EXCURSIONS ..............................................................138

HUELVA, CITY .........................................................................146
HUELVA, EXCURSIONS .........................................................152

Protegemos el bosque; papel procedente de cultivos forestales controlados
Wir schützen den Wald. Papier aus kontrollierten Forsten.
We protect our forests. The paper used comes from controlled forestry plantations
Nous sauvegardons la forêt: papier provenant de cultures forestières controlées

3rd Edition
I.S.B.N. 84-378-1759
Dep. Legal B. 1118-1999